Bygone Lore

John Lord

Alpha Editions

This edition published in 2019

ISBN : 9789389450743

Design and Setting By
Alpha Editions
email - alphaedis@gmail.com

BYGONE BURY

BY

JOHN LORD

Author of "Memoir of JOHN KAY the Inventor of the Fly-Shuttle," and
"Tables for Tensile Strain of Metals"

REPRINTED BY REQUEST FROM A SERIES OF ARTICLES FIRST
PUBLISHED IN THE "BURY TIMES"

Let me review the scene
And summon from the shadowy past
The forms that once have been.
LONGFELLOW.

Rochdale:

JAMES CLEGG, ALDINE PRESS, MILNROW ROAD

1903

RC

m

NOTE.

The reader will find a brief memoir of the Author of Bygone Bury following the Preface in his MEMOIR OF JOHN KAY, *the inventor of the Fly-Shuttle.*

The author was born in Wash Lane, Bury, on April 21st, 1835, and ended his labours on June 27th, 1903.

W. L.

November, 1903.

Contents.

Preface.

HE present volume would not have appeared if the author had not been urged to publish it by several friends. The articles upon "Bygone Bury," were suggested some years ago by a gentleman whose first request was that the writer should say something in the local paper, the *Bury Times*, about "Musical Bury in the last generation," thus an article bearing that title appeared in the issue of December 12th, 1896.

The author's sphere of labour, at that time, was far removed from Bury, and having had for a quarter of a century very exacting and laborious work, travelling in the United Kingdom, he eventually located himself in the northern counties, and though still busy he found ample leisure to think and write about Bury.

The first paper appeared to satisfy the friendly editor of those days, and hints were not only spoken, but written, that something about "Bygone Bury," would be acceptable to the readers. From time to time, as the inspiration came, the following discursive articles were sent to interest whoever cared to spend time over their perusal.

Not inexperienced in newspaper controversy, he endeavoured so to shape his work as to provoke· the fewest imaginable objections. Errors, no doubt, crept in here and there, but "to err is human."

Such as they are, these communications, with some few additions and corrections, once more appeal to an indulgent public, and if sustained interest in the past records of Bury results from these humble reminders, the writer will feel that his efforts have not been in vain.

Should the reader, young or old, incline to dwell upon the strange vicissitudes of life suggested by the events recorded in these reminiscences of " Bygone Bury," and look on present conditions of so-called rich and so-called poor, as anomalous, let this saying be remembered—probably a poor paraphrase culled from "Plutarch's Lives:" "A man is not rich by reason of the abundance of his means, but because of the fewness of his wants."

Few there be who have no love for music. Rich and poor alike are happy under the influence of sweet melody. The early Bury choirs were united under this charm of life. Of these choirs a few opening words are given as a prelude to "Bygone Bury." Lancashire is never wanting in talent, musical and otherwise; may the coming time emulate the past in this respect in the old town of Bury !

Two articles appeared in the *Bury Times* early in 1897, which are here prefixed to "Bygone Bury," in order that the author's incentive and attitude of mind may be the better understood; and the writer of the said articles, will, the author hopes, pardon this re-publication. Subsequently, communications on "Bygone Bury" continued to appear in the *Bury Times* at irregular intervals.

By degrees it became known to the author that his communications to the *Bury Times* had special interest for some of his correspondents—in places far removed from Bury; and applications were made to him for the dates of his earlier papers. Copies of the *Times* containing these papers could not however be supplied, the obvious reason being that provision was not made for such demands. The author hopes, that in the form now presented, the articles may be acceptable to the reader.

OLD BURY.

"My heart untravelled fondly turns to thee."—Goldsmith.

From the *Bury Times*, February 27th, 1897.

"THE recently announced splendid gift of a complete gallery of pictures to the borough of Bury by the present representatives of the Wrigley family, brings to mind some memories of the town and its leading men of almost sixty years ago. Among them, 'laid up in lavender,' figures the founder of the Wrigley dynasty. Familiarly, but not derisively, known as 'Owd Jimmy,' he was the real type of a Lancashire business man of the tough old school, a diamond of the first water not yet submitted to the lapidary. Work, early and late, at 'everything in turns' that came in his way, led to success and established Bridge Hall Mills on a solid basis, even to the third or fourth generation. All honour to the plain, resolute, and indomitable man who did such great things! Slightly lame, but alert and active, he was by force of word and example the inspirer of effort in those about him, and the 'lither' gave him a wide berth. His portrait, if attainable, would give character to the collection of paintings to be some day freely seen by the Technical School students. They could reflect on his career and what he accomplished at a time when helps in education such as are now provided for the children of working men were non-existent, and self-help had to painfully grope if peradventure it might attain its reward.

" Mr. Wrigley's son, ' Tom,' the collector of the pictures, which themselves prove the wealth, taste, and judgment he possessed, was the complete antithesis of his father in appearance, manner, and disposition. He had, of course, the advantage of culture, which circumstances had denied to his father. He was always scrupulously well-dressed, and ' as straight as a picking-rod.' Sanguine in temperament as in complexion, he was imperious and hot in temper as well as fiery by nature. These were the moles sometimes given with the most perfect beauty. But withal though ' terrible in constant resolution,' he was at heart a gentleman, and instinct with many good qualities. In business he excelled—raising Bridge Hall to an eminence it had not before attained. It is said that the *Times* was for a considerable period supplied with their special high-class paper by Mr. ' Tom ' Wrigley's management. In 1861, when the paper duty was abolished without countervailing restriction on foreign paper imported to this country, Mr. Wrigley wrote to the *Times* and denounced the Liberal Government for betraying the important industry with which he was connected. He had hitherto been a free trader, but this one-sided free trade he utterly repudiated. He said we should have the country flooded with foreign paper made from protected materials and by poorly-paid workpeople, and the result would be disastrous to the trade. This outburst was naturally a good deal commented upon, but it had no effect upon legislation. One thing, however, is quite certain, that the flood, small in force at first, has increased in volume year by year, and threatens, as predicted, to submerge the best part of the business. Of the living members of the Wrigley family it would not be pertinent to say more than that they have nobly acted in surrendering their great pecuniary interest in the grand pictures—their heirlooms still in the best sense, though generously dedicated to the use and enjoyment of the inhabitants of Bury for evermore."   N.

OLD BURY.—II.

From the *Bury Times*, March 20th, 1897.

"How often have I paused on every charm !
The sheltered cot, the cultivated farm ;
The never-failing brook, the busy mill,
The decent church that topped the neighbouring hill."
Goldsmith.

"Bury—according to Johnson corrupted from borough, Saxon for dwelling-place—is beautiful for situation and picturesque surroundings. To see these aright a little journey must be made to the high land above Walshaw, on the ridge between Elton and Egerton bottoms in the Bolton valley. From this 'coign of 'vantage' a noble prospect is realised. In the far east a dim outline of Yorkshire and Derbyshire hills is visible—Blackstone Edge, Stanedge, Woodhead, and Kinder Scout. Northward, from Musbury to Knowl Hill, a succession of bold eminences rear their unchanging forms in stately majesty. Holcombe Hill and its Shuttleworth neighbour, like two protecting guardians of the Rossendale forest district, seem to forbid access to that once desolate region. More southerly we see in succession the Birtle, Heywood, and Unsworth uplands, ending with 'the decent church' at Stand, which is a conspicuous and striking object in the general survey. This panoramic sketch imperfectly conveys

the reality of a grand area of some fifty square miles, with all its
intervening variety of detail, comprising towns, villages, hamlets,
and manufacturing works, together with a rural proportion of
farms, fields, gardens, and plantations, which, though now sub-
sidiary to the greater interests of trade, serve to make life more
attractive and alluring, than if the world had become only one
dreary money-making workshop.

> ' 'Tis ours to judge how wide the limits stand,
> Between a splendid and a happy land.'

"Bury, as it is to-day, with its two streams and its busy life,
which like them seems to flow on for ever, couches in the valley
of the Irwell. ' Imagination fondly stoops to trace ' its infant
career from the time when, like a modern back-woodsman, the
first Saxon thane settled on the Irwell, and cleared the land about
his ' dwelling-place.' The everlasting hills looked down upon
him with calm serenity, and the clear, bright streams might sing:

> ' Men may come, and men may go;
> But we flow on for ever.'

And yet, alas! the hills have been roughly handled, and the
streams polluted beyond remedy. We may reasonably suppose
that the country was, in Saxon times, almost if not entirely rough
and wilderness-like in its general character. The streams would
be full of fish, the heron and the kingfisher would revel in the
quiet possession of their native haunts, while the bittern with his
hollow-sounding note would be heard at the breeding season.
There would be extensive swamps, marshes, and bogs in the
lower lands, and the uplands would be moor, forest, and coppice.
Furred and feathered creatures would abound, and Nature would
be king. All this had to be changed. The Saxon settlement
enlarged. Norman accessories added to the energy of expan-
sion, and a town, with its castle for defence of body and its
church for succour to soul, was the result. Trade was gradually

taken up, and woollen weaving introduced. A stimulus to this calling was given in the 14th century by Edward III., who successfully induced Flemish artisans to settle in England. Bury, Bolton, and Manchester welcomed these 'cunning workmen,' who by reason of their skill, industry, and thrifty habits greatly advanced the reputation of Lancashire productions. In the reign of Elizabeth the trade of Bury had become so important that she stationed here an 'Aulnager' (from the French word *aulne*, a measure of length, an ell). This officer had to examine measure, and affix a seal to the cloth. Whether this was done in the interest of the consumer, the producer, or the Government does not appear. The revocation of the Edict of Nantes by the unkingly tyrant, Louis the Fourteenth, in 1685, exiled thousands of the most industrious of the French workpeople, and brought untold misery to many more. As Burns declares—

'Man's inhumanity to man
Makes countless thousands mourn.'

But kings and peasants have the same inevitable end. Their lives are, as the same poet says—

'Like the snowfall in the river,
A moment white—then melts for ever.'

Lives are short, but actions are long in effects. Some of these expatriated Frenchmen came to Lancashire, and it is asserted that Bury had its contingent. Thus, by the cold-blooded barbarity of a misguided king, our commercial supremacy was made more easy of attainment. The tasteful and mercurial Frenchmen added the one little essence of character which completed the Bury idiosyncrasy:

'Describe it who can,
An abridgment of all that is pleasant in man.'

" Until King Cotton came in, woollen ruled in Bury. The inventions of Kay in Bury, and of Crompton and Arkwright else-

where, superadded to the far-reaching steam discoveries of Watt
and others, soon made cotton 'the predominant partner' in
manufacturing circles. Happily Bury, while admitting the new
industry, did not relinquish the old ones. Hence the equability
and permanence of its business firms, whether in woollen,
machinery and iron, paper, or cotton, and the other industries
these involve, such as bleaching, dyeing, printing, &c. But for
a melancholy trade dispute at Walker's machine works some
years ago, it is probable that Bury would have had the place—
a foremost one—now taken by Oldham. However, in spite of
this, Bury has prospered. Its combination of Saxon, Norman,
Flemish, and French ingredients of character has given the solid,
alert, persevering, and ingenious quality which makes for success.
Withal, there is found what phrenologists call adhesiveness.
Love of the old town and its associations is evinced by abiding
in or near it, by adding to its advantages in such ways as parks,
paintings, and other privileges. Moreover, the quality of its
employers and workpeople is shown by the good work turned
out by the town. Bury blankets are famous; Bury paper, from
three leading firms, is equally so—the first for high-class book
and stationery paper; the second for artistic and zephyr-like tints
and crinkled paper; the third for all-round excellence in general
merchants' paper. The cotton goods of Bury have also a world-
wide reputation. Long may Bury endure and flourish!"

                                                        N.

MUSICAL BURY

IN THE LAST GENERATION.

Bury Times, December 12th, 1896.

THERE are no doubt numbers of persons still surviving in Bury whose memories will carry them back to the " fifties " and who can recall the singers of those days. The Crimean war was over; a great weight was removed from the heart of the whole nation. And the people of Bury and the villages round about were provided with a pleasing winter's enjoyment, in the shape of a series of the best concerts ever got up by the united efforts of the Church and Chapel choirs of the town amalgamated, and constituting the Bury Athenæum Choir. The names recently associated with that of the late Mr. Kay Wild will suggest to lovers of music a comparison of opportunities and realisations, then and now. Forty years ago it entailed no little trouble to get up the concerts given to the musically-inclined population. Bury people who could afford the cost were not contented with the quantity provided for them solely in their churches, chapels, or Choral Society; but added to their pleasures by attendance at the Gentlemen's Concerts given at Manchester. The one common bond which held the

people together, enabling them to meet and for the time being
to forget the political contentions of the day, was the innate love
for music.   There is before the writer of these lines, at this
moment, a copy of "Rules and Regulations" of the Bury
Athenæum Choir; attached to the rules is a form of certificate.
The occasion which probably called these rules into concrete
form was an event which no doubt many of the readers of this
notice will recall with special interest — the coming of Sims
Reeves to Bury.   Such events form history in the life of com-
munities, and it seems a pity to let them sink into oblivion.   The
card before the writer sets out : —

Bury Athenæum.

No. 37.   *August 1st, 1856.*

*We certify that John Lord, of Rochdale
Road, Bury, has this day been admitted a
Member of the Bury Athenæum Choir.*

JOHN M. WIKE, Director.

KAY WILD, Secretary.

No doubt these certificates, at the time they were issued, were
highly prized by their recipients.

Richard Hacking, jun., had obtained his degree as Bachelor
of Music at Oxford, and the performance of his Cantata, at the
principal concert of the coming winter, was to take place under
his bâton, himself in his bachelor's robes.   Sims Reeves was to
be the principal attraction among the soloists.   Those respon-
sible for the success of the whole performance, which, besides
the Cantata, was to include " Judas Maccabæus, no doubt felt
desirous of having as perfect a chorus as possible ; and therefore
all members of the chorus respecting whom there was the least

doubt were required to attend an examination before the conductor, Mr. D. W. Banks, who was accompanied by the late Mr. Kay Wild in his capacity as secretary. The examination was held in one of the rooms of the Bury Athenæum, and in carrying it out Mr. Banks presided at a piano. Mr. Banks was a most sympathetic, yet exacting, examiner. And no wonder he was exacting. The success of the whole concert depended upon an intelligent appreciation of the conception in the mind of the composer, to be attempted before the audience only by such as had a fair knowledge of the elements of music as to time and tune. Fugue singing exacted the greatest attention to time; and correct pitch was equally essential, for harmonies and discords required accuracy of ear, in order that the intention of the composer might be realised.

The writer recalls one incident in his own examination, following upon Mr. Banks's rather sudden sternness (assumed, of course, for the occasion) in questioning the candidate. " What do you know about music? And where do you sing on a Sunday? " Somewhat taken aback, the candidate replied to these general questions. Turning over a piece of music which was before him on the piano, " What key is this in? " asked the ruddy-faced, yet kindly and relenting examiner. The correct answer was given. " What time is it written in? " Without hesitation the correct answer was again given. A few other questions and answers; and then, settling himself, to give a fair chance to the timid candidate for the crucial test, the examiner turned over some pages till he came to a piece which required a number of bars to be played by the accompanist, before the vocal notes were called for. That was the awful moment! It was the transition from theoretical knowledge to practical application; a test of the value of voice added to knowledge of how to use it. " Well, now, take up your part in this," said Mr. Banks, and at once commenced his interlude. The purpose in writing this is to refer to a kindly act of appreciation on the part of Mr. Kay Wild, as he sat at his table. His eye caught Mr. Banks's approval, and he was busy writing *before* the singing lesson ended, and the candidate felt he had won! This case throws a light upon the occasion of Dr. Hacking and Sims Reeves's appearance before the Bury public, and how the success of the chorus was attained.

Those were happy days for such as delighted in good music. Among the readers there may be some who recall with amusement their singing lesson:—"A B C D E F G:—H I J K L M N O P:—Q R S T U V:—W X Y Z all right are we." To single out the lovely pieces with which we were made familiar would occupy too many pages. It would not surprise the writer to be told that our Board School method of teaching the alphabet in large classes has been copied from that famous old piece above referred to. It did seem so comical to watch the jovial conductor, as he insisted upon his many pupils intoning the letters of the alphabet, according to his idea of the cadence appropriate. If young children were to be taught their alphabet by this piece of music, it is not improbable that they would learn it in a month perfectly.

Without desiring to be invidious, the writer believes that if asked who were the most musical people in Bury in those bygone days he would have to go among Church people, for the Openshaws and their offshoots, and the Wroes; and among Chapel people for the Wilds, Grundys, Masons, and Kays. No claim is set up in this narrative to exclude other well-informed persons, as the writer only attempts to recall representative people he knew. Mention has been made of a few among the old Choral Society. John Lomax was the son of Ann Openshaw, and he married for his second wife one Ann Openshaw. J. M. Wike was the grandson of Margaret Openshaw, sister to this John Lomax's mother. George Grundy, the brother of Mr. Harry

Grundy, was an enthusiastic organist at Bank Street Chapel for some time; he was grandson of George Openshaw, brother to the mother of John Lomax and to the grandmother of John Melling Wike. Richard Hacking, the composer above referred to, was son of Elizabeth Ann Openshaw, daughter of Samuel Openshaw, of Bolton Street, and his wife Frances Clegg; which Samuel was the son of Thomas Openshaw, of Stanley Street, and his wife Margaret Walker. Richard Hacking, the father of the composer, will be remembered as an enthusiastic musician— the founder of " Hacking's Brass Band," formed among his employees and associates when he was connected with the Walker family, in Butcher Lane.

This takes one's thoughts back to the " forties." About 1842 Hacking's Brass Band was at its best; and the writer has a vivid recollection of the ardour with which at least one member of the band entered on the enjoyment of his labours, in association with the band; for this assiduous endeavour to become proficient in the playing of his part conduced to shorten the days of a beloved uncle. Mrs. Battersby was another descendant of the Openshaws; her mother, or grandmother, would be Ann Openshaw, the daughter of John Openshaw, of Pimhole, and his wife Elizabeth Ormerod. We have seen, in succeeding generations, the branch represented by James Alfred Openshaw, late of Kendal, organist for a time at the Bury Parish Church; and a branch hitherto not named, represented by James Robert Openshaw, professor of music, of Plumtrees. James Alfred Openshaw was the son of James Openshaw, of Beech Hill, Bury, a plain, unassuming man, delighted with nothing so much as with a ramble in the country lanes near Bury and to have a chat with neighbouring farmers; he married twice, the daughters Mary and Sarah of Edmund Bolland, of Heap Brow. James Alfred was the oldest child of Sarah the second wife.

James Robert, the Professor, was the only son of James Openshaw and his wife Mary, daughter of Robert Trimble, of Eden Street. A history of musical Bury should also record the name of Alfred Wroe, the son of Walker Wroe, one of the founders of the Bury Choral Society. He was at one time a singer in Bury Parish Church Choir; afterwards in Bank Street Chapel Choir. The brothers Dennis and Richard Hardman come up clearly in the writer's memory. Dennis Hardman and Kay Wild were contraltos, and almost always seen together. Margaret Hall was in the Church Choir, but, if the writer's memory serves him truly, she was also for a time in the Presbyterian Chapel Choir.

In the report of the funeral of the late Mr. Kay Wild mention is made of some familiar names which, in connection with local musical history, have to the writer, at any rate, some amount of interest. Mr. James Mills recalls to mind the three brothers, John, James, and Thomas, all singers in their day. James and his wife Ellen, the daughter of Mr. Taylor, of Bury, were prominent workers in the Rev. Franklin Howorth's choir, in the Commercial Buildings; and so were Thomas Mills, Richard Fethney, and others. Another name mentioned in the report is that of Mr. Joseph Wrigley, of Walshaw, long ago a familiar face in choir and choral singing. The names of two or three other survivors may be mentioned, and the writer hopes there may be thought no presumption in an outsider doing so—premising that the object is to save from oblivion historical facts as to singers and musicians of the last generation. We still have with us Mr. Thomas Dearden and his esteemed wife Alice, eldest daughter of the late Mr. James Charles, of Bolton Street, Bury; also Mr. Robert Kay, famous in his younger days for the readiness and geniality with which he would gratify his friends by discoursing " The White Squall," and kindred pieces.

The following notice from another pen appeared in the same issue as the foregoing:

THE LATE MR. J. M. WIKE.

DIED DECEMBER 11TH, 1896.

From the *Bury Times*, December 12th, 1896.

Mr. John Mellin Wike, formerly of this town, died at his
residence, 14, Thurlow Road, Hampstead, London, yesterday
morning, in his 63rd year. For some months he had been in
a very precarious state of health, suffering from partial paralysis
and a breaking up of the nervous system. Mr. Wike was the
son of Mr. George Wike, whose father (Mr. John Wike) founded
in the beginning of this century the firm of woollen manufacturers
which in 1838 became known as John Wike and Sons. It is now
nearly 30 years since Mr. Wike left Bury to reside in London.
He was a clever musician and a lover of all that appertained to
music. It has been said of him that he was 'one of the most
liberal and enthusiastic lovers of music that Bury has ever
known.' He was the organist for many years at St. Paul's
Church, and the choir under him attained to a condition of great
proficiency. He was one of the founders of the Bury Choral
Society, which held its earlier meetings at St. Paul's (Bell) School
and afterwards at the Athenæum. Many concerts were given,
and several of Mr. Wike's more successful pupils—for he taught
singing with no inconsiderable success—frequently gave their
services at these concerts. Shortly after he withdrew from the
Choral Society and associated himself with the Bury Musical
Society, the former ceased to exist. He was the prime mover
in all the concerts given by the Choral Society, and for many
years, along with Mr. J. R. Openshaw, of Walmersley Road, took
a very prominent part in the arrangements for the concerts given
by the Musical Society. He was also one of the founders of the
Bury Amateur Dramatic Society, his connection with which he
maintained until 1865, on each occasion acting as musical
director. The last performance in which he took part was when

Mr. Henry Irving came to Bury, on Friday, June 23rd, 1865.
'Hamlet' was on that occasion most successfully staged.
Scenery was painted expressly for the performance by Messrs.
F. W. Livesey and James Shaw (Walmersley Road). In this
play Mr. Wike was musical director. His most intimate friends
at that time were Dr. Banks; Mr. Lawrence Booth, architect;
Mr. J. M. Whitehead, of Helensholme; Mr. Alfred Darbyshire,
architect; and Mr. James Shaw. Mr. Wike was also one of the
small company which built the Prince's Theatre, Manchester, in
1864, with £10,000 capital, under the style of the Manchester
Public Entertainments Company Limited. Twelve months later
the capital was doubled. In 1868 the company was bought up
by a syndicate named the Prince's Theatre Limited, with a
capital of £10,000, and £10,000 mortgage. Of this company
Mr. Wike was elected chairman. Three years later the company
ceased to exist, Mr. Wike and Mr. G. H. Browne jointly buying
out the other shareholders at a small premium. Through the
failure of John Wike and Sons shortly afterwards, the theatre fell
into the hands, as sole proprietor, of Mr. Browne. While in
Bury Mr. Wike was one of the most prominent of local Freemasons. His mother Lodge was St. John No. 191. He had
the reputation of being connected with all the lodges in Bury,
and had passed through the chair of several, including the Prince
of Wales, No. 1012, held at the Derby Hotel. He arranged
most of the dances held by the latter lodge. Several provincial
offices were also held by him. Mr. Wike's mother was a daughter
of Dr. Hardy, of Eckington, Derbyshire. Messrs. G. E. and W.
Wike are his brothers. He leaves a son, John Howard Wike,
who is in America, and a daughter, Grace, who is the wife of
Mr. Freeland, solicitor, London."

And, quite recently, this appreciation has interested many
old singers :

THE LATE MR. W. S. BARLOW.

"The death—March 7th, 1903—of Mr. W. S. Barlow seems to cause the middle of the nineteenth century, and the phases of social life which then distinguished Bury, to recede farther into the past. Mr. Barlow was a member of the old choir of St. Paul's Church, which, under the direction of the late Mr. J. M. Wike, attained a very high degree of proficiency; and one of a small body of singers who, under the late Mr. D. W. Banks, did so much to raise the standard of musical knowledge and attainment in Bury in the fifties. They met first at St. Paul's (Bell) School, but soon adopted the Bury Athenæum as a more centrally situated meeting place, and one less parochial in its character. Even Sir Charles Hallé — he was plain Mr. Hallé then — was glad to make use of the highly-trained nominees of Mr. Banks on occasions when his choir needed augmenting, a fact which speaks volumes for the thoroughness of the methods which this old-time Athenæum conductor adopted.

"Though one of the kindliest and most sympathetic, Mr. Banks was also one of the most exacting of musical directors. There was no chance of an 'inefficient' passing his examination, and the ordeal of question and answer and trial once through, the vocalist felt that he had a standing that would be admitted in the best musical company in the town. Mr. Barlow himself possessed a true bass voice of rare timbre, and by means of close study and strict training he had attained such a degree of technical knowledge as made him master of it.

"The old Athenæum choir had many members, besides their highly-accomplished regular conductor, who were able to wield the bâton and take control of a choir. The successes in this direction of Mr. J. M. Wike and Mr. Kay Wild, director and secretary respectively of the choir, will not be forgotten in Bury for a very long day; and others who were able to undertake the conductor's duties were Mr. D. Hardman, Mr. Richard Hardman, and Mr. W. S. Barlow. The names of these musical men confront us often in reading contemporary records of concerts in Bury in the fifties and sixties, and they recall the first visit of the late Mr. Sims Reeves to sing in the production of the cantata of Mr. Richard Hacking, Mus. Bac., afterwards the Rev. Richard Hacking, Mus. Doc., Rector and organist of Rodbourne, Wiltshire."

Not long ago the writer saw a newspaper cutting from the *Bury Times* of January 29th, 1859, referring to an exhibition of photographic pictures at the Athenæum, in which it was stated, " A number of glees were admirably sung by a select choir, under Mr. W. S. Barlow's direction, Mr. Randle Fletcher and Mr. Spragg rendering efficient service at the pianoforte." It was added that " the fairy fountain was magnificent as ever." This last sentence is a reference to a fountain which at this time was one of the attractions of the Athenæum. In 1856 and 1857 Mr. Barlow's name often figured in the programme of the Athenæum series of cheap concerts, which at the modest prices of 1s., 6d., and 3d., catered for a different class of people from those who attended the more expensive subscription concerts promoted by Mr. D. W. Banks. Sometimes he joined in glees with Miss Margaret Hall, Master H. Nuttall, and Mr. John Allanson. Mr. Barlow continued to be closely associated with music in Bury down to the eighties, and his opinion upon musical matters was held in the highest respect to the last.

BYGONE BURY.

" 'Tis opportune to look back upon old times
and contemplate our forefathers."—*Sir Thomas Browne.*

From the *Bury Times*, April 3rd, 1897.

CHAPTER I.

THERE was another Bury, different from that described in the preceding sketches by " N," which will give readers food for thought. I do not wish unkindly to reflect upon the two papers, but I feel disappointed after perusal of both. Goldsmith's line at the head of the first paper does not express my feelings towards the Bury so described. For one reason, the quotations from other writers, intended to more suitably express the present historian's feelings than he does himself, somewhat annoy my sense of fitness. Then again, as describing the founder of the Wrigley family fortunes, " dynasty " does not beseem the person referred to as " laid up in lavender," or his descendants. They would be the first to disclaim all title to be " a race of kings," and " Owd Jimmy," as I recall him going about the homestead farm at Ash Meadows, was certainly not a type of man I could imagine would be contented to be " laid up in lavender." I may be wrong, but I will hazard the statement that " Bridge Hall " scarcely conveys an accurate description of the scene of

the Wrigleys' early endeavours. Bridge Hall proper was a portion of Grundy's works for worsted spinning and wool-dyeing.
"Bridge Hall Paper Mills" would lead an old Bury native in
idea to "Broad Oak," a good piece of a mile beyond Bridge
Hall.

My earliest recollections go back to my working days at the
waste-picking and white-willowing, about 1843, under the management of Tom Wilson. He was a genial, kindly-spoken person,
liked by young and old. I can yet recall the troubled state of
mind when the Soho took fire in the middle of the day.   It
seemed terrible, the destruction of material and the utter wreck
of the fine structure which occupied a considerable space of
ground in the mill yard. Mr. Thomas Wrigley was at this time
in the very prime of life, and full of energy, quick in temper, but
I believe just in discrimination and decision. He appears to my
memory now, at the head of the stairs leading into the room
where "Old Granny" Howarth and her tribe of youthful waste-
pickers were engaged. One searching glance sufficed, and if
nothing called for remark he would wheel about and depart as
he had come. No place about the Broad Oak Works escaped
his attention. He was a good judge of character, and the *genus*
"skulk" found no abiding-place in any department of his works.
Bridge Hall, the seat of a past member of the Holt family of
Grizlehurst, was at this period occupied by Mr. Edmund Grundy,
junior, who afterwards migrated to Cheetham Hill; and Mr.
Sam. Grundy, then living at Lark Hill, moved to Bridge Hall.

After leaving Bury by the old road to Rochdale, there were
few houses between Topping Fold and Fairfield. Between Fairfield and Broad Oak paper mill there existed, of course, farm-
houses here and there; no other houses besides the row named
Lodge View. On the new road to Rochdale, after passing
"The Seven Stars," things are pretty much as they were, except

as to the rebuilding of Ash Meadows, the residence, subsequently
to his father's death, of Mr. James Wrigley. The future historian may perhaps touch in with a kindly pen the incidents
which contributed to the growth of Bury in those days. The
decadence is equally remarkable. " The Shed " was a busy
scene in woollen manufacture ; and I have heard Thomas Heywood say the woollen trade was so brisk at one period that John
and Edmund Grundy and Co. bought as much to supplement
their own manufactures as they produced at Heap Bridge. In
the time I refer to " The Seven Stars " was known as a sort of
village Parliament house. Its patrons during the occupancy of
" Owd Kester " (Christopher Greenhalgh) were among the local
tradesmen. Between Whitehead Bridge and " The Seven Stars "
there were few houses besides Walker Terrace and Queen Street.
Wike's Lane led into Wash Lane. Midway on the right was Mr.
Thomas Horrocks's residence. His daughter Mary became the
wife of John Lomax Openshaw, the second son of Laurence
Rogers Openshaw, of Brick House. Samuel Horrocks became
an engineer, and removed from his native town. I believe there
was a notice in the *Bury Times* recently of a son of this Mr.
John Lomax Openshaw and his wife Mary, the daughter of Mr.
Thomas Horrocks.

The notice referred to in foregoing is not preserved, but a
more recent one appeared early in the present year, as follows :

A BURY NATIVE'S SUCCESS IN LONDON.

" An appeal has been made to the public in London and to
Masonic Lodges by the Lord Mayor of London on behalf of the
London Hospital, another wing of which the King and Queen
are to open. The Queen has already endowed the wing, and has
taken the greatest interest in this hospital, which is situated in
the East of London where the poor mostly live.

"A correspondent writes :—' It is a pleasure to know that one of the chief surgeons of the London Hospital is Mr. Thomas Horrocks Openshaw, I.M.S., C.M.G., F.R.C.S. Mr. Openshaw is a Bury man, and son of the well-known Mr. J. L. Openshaw, of Heap Bridge, and is related to many of the old Bury families, including Mr. Henry Whitehead, the High Sheriff. Mr. Openshaw left Bury about 20 years ago, after serving some considerable time with the Ramsbottom Paper Manufacturing Co., where he received a severe injury to one of his arms. On going to London to consult a surgeon, he made up his mind to enter the medical profession. Without influence, he has risen to the top of the ladder, is now one of the leading surgeons in London, living at Wimpole Street Home Surgery, and was for many years contemporary of Sir Frederick Treves, of the London Hospital. He was the first surgeon whom the King on his accession honoured with the C.M.G. for services to the poor in London, and also for services in South Africa. Mr. Openshaw went to South Africa for the Government as consulting surgeon : he was captured by De Wet, and was with that General when he routed the Derbyshires, and was left behind. by De Wet to help the wounded and dying. He was for many years in charge of the popular hospital which is situated outside the London docks, and which was an excellent school for a young surgeon, as the number of serious accidents (including broken limbs) average 12 to 15 a day. Mr. Openshaw has also been presented to the Court, and is a regular attender at levees. He was in charge of Buckingham Palace on the Queen's Jubilee, and one of the few recipients who received a silver medal. The King at his Coronation also presented Mr. Openshaw with a Coronation medal. Upon his leaving England for South Africa, hundreds of students gave him a send-off both from Liverpool Street Station and the Docks, carrying him round the Liverpool Street Station shoulder high several times. An exceedingly popular man in the hospital, he is lecturer of anatomy at the London University, and consulting surgeon to the Ormond Street Children's Hospital and to the Surgical Aid Society, a society to enable poor people to procure instruments either free or at a very low cost. Mr. Openshaw is proud of being a Lancastrian and a Bury man especially. He has repeatedly taken the chair at the Lancastrian Society's entertainments, and was W.M. of the Lancastrian Lodge of Freemasons in London for two years.' "

ᐧI believe I am right in saying that the residence of Mr. Thomas Horrocks had formerly been Mr. Wike's, and that fact had given rise to the name "Wike's Lane." I am now referring to the name as current in 1830 and previously, as well as subsequently.

To return to Heap Bridge for a brief space — there was at Ben Mill in those days a venerable man as manager over the carding and slubbing, by name William Leach. One of his daughters became the wife of Mr. Thomas Fairbrother, an intimate friend of Mr. James Smithells, who became the eminent railway manager. Commencing under the East Lancashire directorate—merging into the Lancashire and Yorkshire Railway —he afterwards went to Glasgow to manage the Caledonian Railway. From the same office at Bury went the now eminent railway manager, Sir Myles Fenton. During the construction of the East Lancashire railway and the line from Bury to Castleton, Mr. James Livesey, formerly blacksmith, Heap Bridge, became prominent, as concerned in the work. His daughter Martha became the wife of Mr. James Smithells. Another daughter, Sarah, became the wife of Mr. Arthur Bentley, who started the small iron foundry, in Wike's Lane, which was afterwards occupied by Livesey and Ashton as caddy sheet weavers. After Mr. William Ashton relinquished work there, Mr. John Hamer (who had left Walker and Lomax, and had been manager for a time of the mill, then recently erected by the late Mr. Charles Edward Lomax—now J. K. Schofield and Co. Limited) carried on cotton manufacturing.

The inception of Co-operative or Joint Stock manufacturing was doubtless the work of the village Parliament held at "The Seven Stars," Little Bridge. There, in the little snug, would assemble for "nightcaps" and smoke, a few who became active in the formation of the Bury and Heap Commercial Company. There would be Mr. Samuel Kay, of Wash Lane, hatter; Mr. James Livesey, of Heap Bridge; Mr. Edmund Bridge, who had succeeded Mr. Livesey at the smithy at Heap Bridge; Mr. George Smith, of Heap Bridge; Mr. John Greenhalgh, son of Christopher, the old "boniface" of "The Seven Stars." These names will all be found as those of the most active promoters of the new company. Mr. John Lightbown, grocer, of Freetown, was another. [The author's identity for obvious reasons, was somewhat hidden in the initials. But under their new dress there no longer need be secrecy. The first Secretary to the Bury and Heap Commercial Company was the present Author. And he is informed that the Share Certificates of the first shares still bear his signature. And so far as the Bury and Elton Manufacturing Company was concerned, the Author, at request of Mr. Thomas Barlow, put that new Company's books in correct order; and produced the first balance sheet for the first meeting of shareholders]. The Lancashire Waggon Company had then become a great success, and it was quite reasonable that if out-siders could conduct a successful business, even without a work-shop, in supplying rolling stock to railway companies and coal agents and others, the like enterprising spirit would succeed in the cotton trade. So rose up the Bury and Heap Commercial Company, whose shareholders were found far and near. Rochdale people showed great confidence in the men at the head of the new venture. Heywood people also. Then sprang up the Bury and Elton Manufacturing Company, at the old mill vacated by Mr. John Walker, in Elton. At the formation of this latter company the experience of an old manufacturer was of great value, in the person of Mr. Thomas Barlow, who for a long period was manager of Brickhouse Mill after cotton became the staple wrought there. Mr. Thomas Barlow will be recalled to mind as subsequently the head of the paper-woollen business, with his son, Mr. Micah Barlow, who was in his youthful days one of Bury's crack cricketers.

In this brief notice you will find names of many who have had no mean share in the past successes of trades in Bury. But if we investigate the history of Bury trade for a generation or two further back it will be found that the enterprising spirit of the townsfolk was no mean adjunct to the renown of their county generally. The Openshaws, Hutchinsons, Walkers, Grundys, Ashtons, Rothwells, Kays, all come into view. Of some of these I purpose jotting down some traditionary items and recollections in the hope that they may fill up gaps in local history which seem like voids that ought not to remain, if we are to take a place worthy our deserts in the future. It has been the case in the past of Bury that money-making has appeared to be the principal end in life. Historians have been struck with the fact that seldom has one risen to the occasion to recount the facts worth noting. The cause of this may be found in the fact that as a town we have had a plethora of talent, with an accompanying disinclination to exercise it for the benefit of future generations.

BYGONE BURY.

CHAPTER II.

From the *Bury Times*, April 10th, 1897.

FOLLOWING my last paper, I may continue reference to some names not yet entirely forgotten by old residents of Bury and neighbourhood; for down the stream of Time memory is to these readers the only source of real enjoyment of life. Experience, recollections of participation in scenes remembered in early life, we often find to be an endless round of enjoyment to these survivors of "Bygone Days." What life was then cannot possibly be imagined by the present generation. Pictures may be thrown on the screen, and vivid descriptions given by pen or tongue; but all come short of pourtraying to young people of this day the actual life.

Two generations have passed since Bridge Hall Paper Mills were worked by Messrs. Wrigley and Nuttall. I have no trace of the branch of the Nuttall family which went into partnership with the Wrigley firm, subsequent to J. and F. Wrigley. Was it not a "Squire Nuttall" whose death was the opportunity which James Wrigley took for establishing the firm subsequently so widely known as James Wrigley and Sons? The period I refer to would be the latter days of hand-loom weaving. Power-looms would be only just heard of at this time. We find James Wrigley and Son, dimity, quilting, and fustian manufacturers, 22, Fleet Street, Bury; and James Wrigley and Son, bleachers and spinners, at Gigg Mill. The old water-power mill at Gigg was the place where yarns were prepared for weaving in the cottage loom-houses round the neighbourhood.

One family to which Bury owes much of the prosperity enjoyed during the past sixty or seventy years sprang from the firm of William Walker and Sons, woollen manufacturers, Stanley Street. To give readers some idea of how this came about I must go into some genealogical particulars. In seeking for causes of change in a given locality we sometimes discover the key to some family history—a key to unlock the repository containing the explanation of causes and consequences we otherwise should fail to comprehend. I do not propose to lay emphasis upon the points in my narrative which throw the light upon subsequent events. A " tree " genealogically grown up, which should show the trade of Bury as it was evolved out of the elements of energy and capital in the early years of this century, would be a most remarkable tree. The rootings and graftings, the foliage and branches, the vigorous trunk and the decaying tops, along with prominent branches, would be a marvellous picture. My readers will be surprised, probably, that I should have to say there is only one stem of this composite tree indigenous to Bury soil, strictly speaking. To the elucidation of the suggested picture, I should say one stem will have been brought from Whitefield; another came from Burnley district; another, or perhaps two, came from Bolton and district. From these various localities there appeared, as time marched on, such combinations of families as resulted in our past prosperity and pomp. I must carry the minds of my readers back into the misty past, when Moorside was actually the outer edge of the moors. Probably there would be then only a few straggling houses between the end of Walmersley Lane and the ancient Parish Church. From the Parish Church to Bury Bridge would be the narrow old Mill Lane. Water Street, Stanley Street, Rock Street, and Fleet Street would be a sequence of windings and turnings, so to speak, a map of which would be amusing to the pupils in the modern Technical School. This tortuous line of houses would end at the old Bury Cross, which stood on the spot now occupied by Peel's monument. Much of the trade of Bury, in those old days, was carried on in the stretch of houses I have named.

For the purpose of my present paper I must go back still further; and I do so in order to make clear the connections traceable between the present and the past. I find myself among the records of the turbulent epoch, about the time of Oliver Cromwell. Peter Ormerod, of Ormerod, in the County of Lancaster, was the son and heir of Laurence, the twelfth in descent from Matthew de Homerode, living 55 Henry III. I name this Peter because he was the son of Elizabeth, the daughter of Robert Barcroft of Barcroft, and his wife Elizabeth, the daughter of John Roberts, of Foxstones. These localities have all a special interest to antiquaries, and, as will shortly appear, are also of interest to Bury readers of to-day. Peter Ormerod, above named, was twice married. His first wife was Jennet, daughter of John Howarth, of Monton, in Eccles; and it is with George Ormerod, the fourth son of this marriage, I am firstly concerned. He married Annie Pilling, of Eccles. The issue of this marriage, three sons and two daughters, are recorded—Laurence, Oliver, Peter, Elizabeth, and Annie. Laurence died during his father's lifetime, without leaving issue. Oliver and Peter came to reside in Walmersley and Bury. This Oliver Ormerod married twice. Alice, the daughter of Charles Howarth, of Chatterton Hey, Tottington, was his second wife. Married in 1704 and dying

25th June, 1740, she left one son and four daughters. Oliver, her husband, survived to a great age; born in 1672, he outlived his second wife 28 years, and paid Nature's debt in 1768. Their only son, George, married Anne, the daughter of John Hutchinson, of Bury. This George was born 1719, and dying 29th June, 1789, was buried at St. John's Chapel, Bury. I believe he was the youngest child of the above-named Oliver Ormerod. Elizabeth, probably the eldest of Oliver Ormerod's daughters, married 28th October, 1725, John Openshaw, of Pimhole. They had five sons and two daughters. Mary, the eldest of these girls, married Henry Butterfield, of Bury. This Mary was born 7th December, 1732. In the early years of this century there were two persons of this name in business in Bury, viz., James Butterfield, linen draper, and shoe dealer, Fleet Street, and Thomas Butterfield, shuttlemaker, near Stanley Street. Presumably these were sons of Henry Butterfield and his wife Mary Openshaw. Ann, the sister of this Mary, was born 17th February, 1735, and married 11th June, 1753, to Robert Battersby, of Bury. Many readers will recognise this family name. I can recall the old house this family occupied, fifty years ago, in Parsons Lane. One of the earliest Bury Improvement Commissioners is recorded as Robert Battersby, junior, who sat for the years 1847, 1848, 1849, and 1850. He was engaged in the woollen manufacture.

I must now take the sons of the afore-mentioned Ormerod-Openshaw wedding. The eldest, James, born 1726, died 1835. John, the second son, born 1729, died 1781; his wife, Betty, survived till 1801. I find three daughters born of this couple— the wife of George Holt, of Starkies; the wife of Richard Kay, of Limefield; and Jane the wife of William Norris. The third son of the Ormerod-Openshaw marriage was Thomas Openshaw, of Stanley Street, Bury, who married first Margaret Walker (of whom further mention will be made), and, second, Sarah Powell.

The fourth son was George, named " George of Seals ; " and the
fifth son was James Openshaw of Redvales. This George, " of
Seals," remained at Pimhole, and his wife was Elizabeth Heywood. Of their family we must treat after a brief return to
Peter Ormerod of Ormerod, who married for his second wife
Margaret Ormerod; in all probability this was a marriage of
cousins. The issue traced of this second marriage has especial
interest for many persons in Bury. It will throw light upon the
family history and names of many of the most eminent townsfolk.
The record available to the writer shows one son born to Peter
Ormerod, of Ormerod, and his second wife, Margaret Ormerod,
viz., Oliver Ormerod, of Foxstones. Foxstones estate probably
came into the Ormerod family, as indicated above, by the marriage of Elizabeth Roberts with Robert Barcroft, whose daughter
Elizabeth was the mother of this Peter Ormerod. Be that as it
may, we have Oliver Ormerod, of Foxstones, marrying Mary
Spenser. Their son Laurence married Mary Halsted, whose
son, Oliver Ormerod, married Elizabeth Hartley; of which last
wedding we find two sons, William and John, recorded. William,
the eldest of these two, of Foxstones, was baptised in 1717. He
married Sarah Lord (probably the daughter of John Lord, of
Broadclough, in Rossendale). Of this marriage I have record of
one son and two daughters. This son, Oliver Ormerod, was never
married, but his namesake is represented to-day, by the son of his
godchild, in the person of the esteemed Mayor of Bury (1897)
Alderman Oliver Ormerod Walker, J.P. This brings me back
to ancient Stanley street, in Bury. There was once a firm styled
William Walker and Sons, woollen manufacturers, Stanley Street.
William Walker, at the head of this firm, married Mary Ormerod,
the daughter of William Ormerod, of Foxstones. I may incident-
ally say that this William Walker was the son of Richard Walker,
of Stone Pale Farm, and his wife, Rachel Grundy, of Balding-

stone. And, also, let me here say that Margaret Walker, who became the wife of Thomas Openshaw, of Stanley Street, was sister of this Richard, of Stone Pale Farm.

The reader has, in the foregoing, evidence as to how Bury became noted as " a good market town." The Ormerods, Openshaws, Walkers, Hutchinsons, Grundys, Kays, and Battersbys were all eminent in trade. What does the " town and trade " of Bury owe to the offspring of the last-named wedding from Foxstones? The mere enumeration of the sons of William Walker and his wife Mary (Ormerod) will be sufficient to lead older readers to ask " how much ! "

Since the above was written the Author has met with the following note by Canon Raines, which carries this family back a few generations :

17 Aug. 1753.

𝕵𝖓𝖉ᵗ betw Rt. Hon. Edward Earl of Derby 1ᵖᵗ and Richard Walker of Bury Co. Lancs. 2ⁿᵈ pᵗ Recites the Surr. of a Lease date 22 July 1719 wherein is in being the life of Mary Guy & of Surr. of another Indᵗʳ dated 3ʳᵈ April 1713 Wherein are in being the lives of Jonathan Lees and Elizabeth Walker and also of Surr. of anothʳ Lease date 1ˢᵗ Oct. 1718, wherein are in being the lives of John Holt & Richard Holt and also the sum of £314 sᵈ Earl lets all that Tent in Unsworth called Parr's being a house and housing & outhouse, 15 bays & land there, and in Whitefield, being 29a. 1r. op. large measure, 8 yds. to rod, in the manor of Pilkington sᵈ Co. now in tentᵗ sᵈ Richard Walker, except Woods, Mines, Free Warren, Birds and Beasts of Free Warren with libʸ for Earl his heirs and assigns to enter Hunt Hawk and Kill Game and take all Fish and Wild Fowle & Enclose Wastes within said manor To have &c. for lives of Richard Walker age 19 and John Walker aged 3 years, sons of sᵈ Richard, and George son of James Holt of Bury Innkeeper at 4 yʳˢ Rent £1 2s. od. and to keep a Dog and a Cock, and plant 20 young Trees of Oak, Ash, or Elm yearly.

D

This Lease of 1753 will be found to refer to the Richard
Walker, the great-grandfather of the first Member of Parliament
for Bury. It was this Richard, aged 19 in 1753, that married
Rachel Grundy.

On the 17th April the following appeared in the *Bury Times*:

NOTE :—" Mr. Jeffrey P. Nuttall, Frecheville Place, Bury, writes:
' Referring to an account of Bygone Bury in last Saturday's *Bury
Times*, in which your contributor says he has ' no trace of the
branch of the Nuttall family which went into partnership with
the Wrigley firm '— the Nuttall referred to was not Squire
Nuttall, as he supposes, but was John Nuttall, son of Robert
Nuttall, of Top-o'th'-Lee, Shuttleworth. The partnership was
entered into in 1820 for a term of seven years. After the dis-
solution of partnership John Nuttall commenced business on his
own account as a paper manufacturer at Heap Bridge. He died
on the 18th February, 1837, aged 47 years. His two surviving
sons, Robert Nuttall, of York House, Whitefield, and John
Nuttall, of the address at the head of this letter, are well known."

BYGONE BURY.

CHAPTER III.

From the *Bury Times*, April 17th, 1897.

WITH regard to the marriage of William Walker and Mary Ormerod — the former, head of the firm of William Walker and Sons, woollen manufacturers, Stanley Street, Bury; the latter, daughter of William Ormerod, of Foxstones—I have records of six sons and four daughters. Richard Walker, the first representative of Bury in Parliament, was the first-born of this marriage. He married Ann, daughter of John Scholes, of Bury, of whose issue I have records of Richard, of Bellevue; John Scholes, of Limefield; William; Mary, who married Mr. Vance, of Blackrock, Co. Dublin; Anne, wife of the Rev. Henry Ainslie; and Jane, wife of Colonel Roberts, of the 4th Regiment of Foot. After Richard, Member of Parliament, I find Samuel Grundy Walker, who died unmarried, and then I come to Oliver Ormerod Walker, the favourite and godchild of his bachelor uncle above referred to, and whose name he received. Who among the residents of Bury will fail to recall the gentleman I here refer to? His affable, dignified, gentle demeanour, even to the lowliest of his workpeople, endeared him to all. He was really the type of " a fine old English gentleman," as I recall him. William Walker was the fourth son. The two brothers, William and Oliver Ormerod Walker were co-partners with John Lomax, of

Springfield, in the firm of Walker and Lomax, of Moor Side
Works, of which more may be written yet. We have one other
brother to mention, John Walker, who commenced the extensive
works in Elton, subsequently occupied by the joint-stock company named the Bury and Elton Commercial Company. Of the
daughters of William Walker and his wife Mary, of Foxstones,
Sarah became the wife of John Hutchinson, and Rachel married
William Harper, solicitor. I have mentioned the marriage of
Richard, the Member of Parliament. His brother William
married Jane Judith, daughter of William Calrow, and John
Walker married Catherine, the daughter of Samuel Holker.

Here we have other old Bury firms brought into our narrative—William and Thomas Calrow, merchants and cotton spinners, Woodhill; Samuel Holker, woollen manufacturer, Millgate;
and Thomas and John Hutchinson, woollen manufacturers, Silver
Street. I am unable to follow, further than the mention of the
only son of the above Oliver Ormerod Walker, namely, the
present chief magistrate of Bury, Colonel Oliver Ormerod Walker.
Returning to the earlier marriage into the Ormerod family, we find
ourselves again in Stanley Street, at the house of Thomas Openshaw, the third son of John of that ilk, of Pimhole, and Elizabeth,
the daughter of Oliver Ormerod, of Walmersley, before named.
Here we have the clue to the Christian names " Oliver Ormerod "
Openshaw and " Ormerod " Openshaw, names met with in two
separate branches of this family. There are many descendants
surviving in Bury of this first marriage of Thomas Openshaw
and his wife, Margaret Walker. They had a very numerous
family. This Thomas Openshaw was, as stated, twice married,
and of the second marriage you have Charles Openshaw, the
founder of " Owd Charley's," Butcher Lane. The two families
born to Thomas of Stanley Street numbered upwards of twenty
sons and daughters. In tracing the history of this family, we

discover the only surviving firm (in the sole proprietorship of a member of the Openshaw family), is the cotton spinning and manufacturing carried on in Elton by James Henry Openshaw, whose wife is daughter to Joseph Newbold, a former employer of labour in Bury. In 1818 there was Joseph Newbold, millwright, engineer, and manufacturer of wrought-iron, steam boilers, &c., and smiths' work of all descriptions, Rock Street. Subsequently this business was carried on in Paradise Street, by the first-named Joseph Newbold. To trace the connections of these early business men in Bury is interesting. During the early years of the Pimhole branches of woollen manufacturing, it was quite natural that there would be offshoots transplanting themselves away from the parent stock. Hence we find Thomas, of Stanley Street. He had a son, John Openshaw, who married a first cousin, Alice, the daughter of George " of Seales." This Alice was the eldest daughter of George Openshaw and his wife Elizabeth Heywood. To enumerate the children of this family is once more to remind readers of what the " town and trade " of Bury owe to the enterprising spirit derived from the Ormerod-Openshaw union. We have, then, Alice, as named, marrying John, her cousin, of Stanley Street. Of this and what it led to we shall find more to say. Rachel, the next child, married a Pilkington ; Elizabeth, the next after Rachel, died unmarried. Mary, the fourth daughter, married her cousin, William Walker Openshaw, of Eden Street. John Openshaw, the eldest son, married Mary, the daughter of John Topping, of Topping Fold, Bury; Ann, the sixth-born, married John Lomax, of Barrack Fold, Ainsworth, of whom it will also be interesting to relate some facts regarding the trade of Bury. Margaret, the seventh child, married John Wike, of Croft House. George, the second son, and eighth and last child, remained only a brief period at Pimhole. Leaving the parental roof, he began life for himself at Brickhouse.　He married Mary, the daughter of Richard Booth, of Pits-o'-th'-Moor.　In the above series of names it will again be readily seen how much the trade of Bury was influenced by this family.　Herein we discover the origin of four new firms. John Openshaw of Stanley Street, with his wife Alice of Pimhole, set up housekeeping and started business at Starkies, Manchester Road—all statements to the contrary notwithstanding.　There is no need to dwell upon this assertion, beyond remarking, for the benefit of subscribers to the voluminous pedigree published a few years ago, that this branch of the family pedigree is admitted by the compiler of the volume mentioned, to be imperfect, by reason of paucity of information procurable before publication.　However, from this marriage of Alice with her cousin John, and also through the marriage of Ann, the sister of this Alice, with John Lomax, of Barrack Fold, we come to some incidents affecting the trade of Bury, as we shall see further on.

John Openshaw, last-mentioned, who settled at Starkies, carried on woollen cloth manufacturing.　But there was competition to be reckoned with in those days, as ever since.　His uncle George " of Seales " was carrying on a similar business at Pimhole.　John at Starkies had rather an uphill job before him. He was, however, a man of kindly nature, and willing to help a poor fellow in need, as the following little incident will show. Many readers will be acquainted with the romantic history of a subsequently famous family who came southward in search of fortune ; and, as tradition affirms, surveyed the scenes of their future successes from the hill-top now crowned with the memorial known as Grant's Tower — on the eminence opposite stands a further monument, bearing the name of another enterprising family which came down the same valley and also helped to make Bury notable in the manufacturing world.　The men of Scotia trudged their way on to Bury, making, no doubt,

as historians say, for Hampson Mills. They found themselves
benighted on reaching the homestead of John and Alice Openshaw at Starkies. They craved food and lodgings, and obtained
both. The then five-year-old son of John and Alice Openshaw
used to relate in his old age this incident of his childhood's
days—how his mother sent him with supper for the strangers,
and how his father bade him help them to needful straw for a
shakedown bed. Another incident he would also relate with
pride—the ownership of a pony his parents humoured him with.
This indulgence might be the emulation of pride of birth; but
fate willed it to be of brief duration. In 1782 there came a
change of fortune, and removal from Bury ensued. John Openshaw obtained a very lucrative position in Birmingham, with a
brewer and distiller. His wife left the scene of their reverses.
In the last journey her husband made homeward he called at
the hostelry of his cousin Dawson at Whitefield, where he caught
a chill, which had increased in virulence by the time he reached
home, and after a short illness he died. This was some years
after they had left Bury. The widow, Alice, returned to Pimhole
with her family, now increased to four or five, of which her three
boys are concerned, more or less, with our history of the bygone
tradefolk of the town. Alice was a woman of high spirit, strong
will, and great independence of character—qualities which had
not a little influence upon the future of some of the more recent
firms in Bury. Her sister Ann also, through her children, exhibited so wise a discrimination as to conduce to further in-
fluencing and moulding the destinies of some of the large
establishments in the town. Alice, the widow just named, had
three sons— James the eldest, John the next, and Thomas the
youngest. Of the descendants of James, John (the eldest) was
some time in the service of the late Richard Hacking, at Heaton
Grove; George was for years in the cotton waste trade; Henry
was in early life the cashier and outrider for Simpson, Bland, and

Howarth. These, with a sister, Sarah, who married William
Shaw, of North Street, were the children of James by his first
marriage.   He married a second time, Ann, the daughter of
Robert Shepherd and his wife Ellen Kay, of " Cobbas," who
farmed the " Seales " farm at Pimhole.   Of this marriage there
were one daughter and two sons, Rachel (of whom the author is
the eldest son), James, and William.

In the family of John Openshaw, the second son of the
widowed Alice, there were several sons who made their mark in
the trade of Bury.   James, the eldest of these, will be remembered as latterly partner in the firm of Walker and Lomax ; and
his representatives remain, as the townsfolk will know ; Thomas
was with John Walker up to the period of commencing on his
own account the spinning of cotton in the Mosses ; Joshua was
at one time, I believe, with Joseph Newbold, and subsequently
developed a good business in oils and tallow—he married Elizabeth, the only child of his cousin George Openshaw ; Ormerod
Openshaw died comparatively a young man, leaving sons still in
Bury.   Of Thomas, the third child left with the widowed Alice,
only one child, a daughter, survived him—Ann, who became the
second wife of John Lomax, son of Ann, her father's aunt.   And
thus readers of a genealogical turn may see how the family tree
would grow and become intertwined.   George Openshaw (the
younger of the two sons of George " of Seales,") began the
manufacture of woollen cloth at Brickhouse, sometime previously
to the year 1818 ; we find in the Lancashire General Directory
for 1818 that he was then at Brickhouse.   Probably in anticipa-
tion of contemplated change, he built the house of bricks, hence
the place-name.   His father was carrying on the same kind of
business in Butcher Lane.   His brother John remained at Pimhole, founding ultimately the firm of John Openshaw, Sons,
and Co.   George was married in 1796 ; and we find records of
one son and four daughters born of this marriage.   In the Will

and accompanying settlement of her affairs, Ann Lomax (named earlier on), sister of George, who settled at Brickhouse, mentions with special favour her son John of Springfield, and her daughter Eleanor Lomax. John Lomax was then a cotton manufacturer, 39, Stanley Street, Bury, and " put out " warps and weft to hand-loom weavers, as forty years ago I often heard his old servant John Hunt relate. And here comes in the natural order of our narrative, that fact that the only surviving daughter of John Hunt married John Henry Openshaw, the eldest son of Henry, who was with Simpson, Bland, and Howarth.

John Openshaw (who as just stated was the head of the firm of John Openshaw, Sons, and Co.) and his wife Mary, the daughter of John Topping of Topping Fold, had five sons and five daughters. John the eldest, born 1782, married a Miss Lord, but died childless. George the second son resided at Roach Bank (probably built for him), and he married Margaret Ramsbottom of Birtle. Ultimately he went to reside at Stony Hill, Southport. Thomas, known among his loving and beloved neighbours and the poor of Pimhole as " Mr. Thomas " or " Owd Mr. Tummy," has left his mark in several ways and places. His intense earnestness and endeavour for the benefit of his work-people was ever a distinguishing feature of his character. The school at Pimhole, St. Paul's Church, the monumental church at Pimhole, and the munificent charities left by his Will to Bury churches and charities, will ever keep green the memory of an unassuming personality. He was a bachelor, and at Primrose Hill, Pimhole, had with him his two spinster sisters, Richmal and Rachel.

Oliver Ormerod, the fifth and last son of the family, I will here name out of his natural order, for the reason that to suit my narrative, I may refer more fully to James the fourth son. Oliver Ormerod married Dorothy, daughter of John Greenhow of Kendal—sister of Mrs. Grundy of Bankfield, whose husband,

Thomas, was head of the noted firm of Thomas, Alfred, and
John Grundy, solicitors. Here we have another family connection blending various bygone notables. Bury has received one
memorable token of sympathy from a good-natured son of this
marriage, in the gift of the park or playground at Pimhole—the
giver, Thomas Ormerod Openshaw, of recent memory. I will
pass on now to James the fourth son, above referred to. Plain,
unassuming, and careless of the world's comments, he would put
on " wooden shoon " for a ramble out in the lanes leading from
his house at Beechhill, by Gigg and Pilsworth farms, and round
about, home again. He had met his fate at the fireside of
Edmund Bolland's house, Heap Brow, and was married to Mary
Bolland on the 19th June, 1823. They had born to them two
sons and two daughters. John Ormerod Openshaw, the first-
born child, was baptized at St. John's Church, Bury, 20th June,
1824 ; and on the 2nd December, 1852, he married Alice, the
daughter of Joshua Knowles. She was born 2nd June, 1823.
Of this union I find record of one son, James, born 19th October,
1853, and called away at the early age of twenty years, January
21st, 1873. A daughter, Jane, born in May, 1826, survived only
about two years. Sarah Openshaw, the last of the children of
Mary (Bolland) Openshaw, was born 9th March, 1831 ; and
married 9th July, 1862, John Bradbury, M.D., F.R.C.P., of
Cambridge, who was born 27th February, 1841. And then,
in 1833, Mary was called away by the dread summons. James
Openshaw then sought for sympathy and help a second time at
the same fireside where he found his first wife, Sarah Bolland
taking her sister Mary's place on the 12th October, 1835. Sarah
was the mother of James Alfred Openshaw, Mary Ann Openshaw, and Arthur Albert Openshaw. This Mary Ann Openshaw
married William Ormerod Walker, son of the senior partner of
Walker and Lomax, and cousin in first degree to Colonel O. O.
Walker, now Mayor of Bury. Readers cannot fail to observe the

persistence with which " Ormerod " held the families referred to. There comes a period when the healing hand of time leads the sorrowing to dwell less on the past, and more upon present duties and responsibilities. Some such change came over John Ormerod Openshaw's sorrowing widow, who became the wife of Dr. Davies, a name associated with loving deeds for the benefit of the women of Bury.

The County Borough of Bury, in the County Palatine of Lancaster, of the year 1897, differs so much from the Bury of 1837, in all directions—it seems as if you are under some enchanter's wand. You are making history at a marvellous rate. This is a digression I could not resist after reading your paper of April 3rd. One's thoughts go back to the pitiless days in the hard times which were the lot of the day labourers of sixty years ago. Why, to the children of those days a stick of slate pencil was a positive treasure ; a blacklead pencil was the envy of every lad who could not indulge in a copper to buy one ; paper— writing paper—was even more precious to the struggling youth of that time.

NOTE.—John and Alice Openshaw named in this chapter united in their marriage the Openshaws of Pimhole and Stanley Street. For a generation or two the burial place of this John was a mystery to the family. Such, at anyrate, was the information conveyed to the author. In the latter part of April, 1903, the author discovered a gravestone in Bury Parish Churchyard which undoubtedly gives the long desired particulars.

"Joseph the son of John and Alice Openshaw of Redvales died 1784 aged 2 years."

"John Openshaw died 23 July 1790 aged 39 years."

" Elizabeth their daughter died 1797 in her 20th year."

" Alice the wife of John Openshaw died May 18 1812 aged 58 years."

The Openshaw Pedigree published a few years ago is somewhat incomplete as to this branch of the family. There was mutual regret expressed between the author of that Pedigree and the present writer that they had not sooner met.

BYGONE BURY.

THE KAYS.

CHAPTER IV.

THE town and trade of Bury suffered much in years long past from popular ignorance and blindness; in no instance more than in the treatment of John Kay and his son Robert, whose inventions have done so much for the world. Shuttles, reeds, and cards were so greatly modified by these far-sighted men as to entirely change the methods of spinning fibrous material and weaving cloth. Bury raised a monument to the statesman who made large loaves possible out of the means formerly absorbed in procuring small loaves. Bury should raise a monument to commemorate the inventions of the two Kays.

In the *Gentleman's Magazine* for 1867 there is a paper (vol. iii., p. 336) upon "Monuments to Public Benefactors." After one or two cases in point the writer says:

"But perhaps no more striking instance of such neglect is exhibited than in the case of the two Kays—John and Robert, father and son, of Bury, Lancashire. John invented the extended lathe, fly-shuttle, and picking-peg, together with woollen and cotton carding engine, the original model of which is in the possession of Thomas Oram, Esq., of Bury, his grandson. Robert, his son, invented the wheel-shuttle and drop-box. John's history is a melancholy one. Educated abroad, where he acquired a taste for mechanics, he came to England and set up a woollen manufactory at Colchester, previously marrying the daughter of John Holt, Esq., of Bury, to which place he afterwards moved, and where he made these inventions. The reception he met with verified the old prediction respecting prophets, &c., and he was obliged to flee to Paris, where he died ' a heart-broken exile,' and no trace of him has ever been discovered."

It was in the year 1733 that John Kay invented the fly-shuttle and picking-peg. Baines in his *History of the Cotton Manufacture*, says :

" Mr. Kay brought this ingenious invention to his native town, and introduced it among the woollen weavers in the same year, but it was not much used among the cotton weavers until 1760. In that year Mr. Robert Kay, of Bury, son of Mr. John Kay, invented the drop-box, by means of which the weaver can at pleasure use any one of three shuttles, each containing a different coloured weft, without the trouble of taking them from and replacing them in the lathe."

Baines derives his information from Mr. Guest, who had written a *History of the Cotton Manufacture*, getting his information from a manuscript lent to him by Mr. Samuel Kay of Bury, son of Mr. Robert Kay the inventor of the drop-box. In a directory for 1818 I find mention of Samuel Kay, gentleman, 27, Union Square, and Samuel Kay, gentleman, 44, Fleet Street; also Samuel Kay, farmer, 24, Stanley Street. The Samuel Kay of 27, Union Square, I find in another directory for 1824-5, recorded as cotton manufacturer; and as the Samuel Kay of Fleet Street does not again appear, I assume he was dead or had

removed. He was the person named by Guest. Another account says :

"In the year 1738 John Kay (a relation of the celebrated Dr.
Fletcher), a native of Bury, introduced the means of throwing
the shuttle by means of the picking-stick instead of by hand, and
hence called the fly-shuttle. In consequence of the fury of the
populace he was compelled to remove to Colchester."

Harland has it thus :

"In 1738 John Kay, a native of Bury, but at this time of
Colchester (to where he had fled from mob-usage at Bury), invented a new mode of throwing the shuttle (in weaving), by
means of the picking-peg ; and in 1760 Robert Kay, son of the
foregoing, invented the drop-box for looms. Setting cards also
belong to these two Kays of Bury."

A fuller account, and more accurate I think, which has been
compiled from various sources, states that John Kay was born at
Park, Walmersley, near Bury, 16th July, 1704. Some writers
refer to him as "Kay of Bury," to distinguish between him and
a Warrington clockmaker named John Kay, who was associated
with Arkwright in the inventions of spinning machinery. It
would be interesting to trace the clockmaker's origin. Our Kay
is said to have been educated abroad. When he came back
from school his father, who had a woollen mill at Colchester,
placed him in charge of it. But he could not have been very
successful there, for we find that when he was about twenty-six
years of age he was settled in Bury as a reedmaker, and in that
year, 1730, took out his first patent (No. 515) for "an engine for
making, twisting, and carding mohair, and twining and dressing
of thread." The sequel proves that what Bury lost Saltaire and
Paisley gained. About this period (1730) he also discerned a
substitute for cane splits, in the rolling and polishing flattened
wire, for reed-dents. These flat-wire dents could be made

thinner and smoother than cane-splits, and fabrics of much finer and more even texture could be woven thereby. Then, in 1733, his fly-shuttle was patented (No. 542). By its use a weaver could easily double his former quantity of work, and equally increase its quality. In this same patent (542, 1733) was included a machine for batting wool for removing dust from it by beating sticks. In 1738 the inventor's active mind conceived a method of utilising windmills for working pumps, and he took out a patent in that year for his windmill-pump (No. 561). He called himself in this windmill specification an engineer. Woodcroft, in his *Brief Biographies of Inventors*, says that in this year, 1738, John Kay moved to Leeds. The new shuttle was largely adopted by the woollen manufacturers of Yorkshire, but they were unwilling to pay royalties, and an association called the Shuttle Club was formed to defray the costs of legal proceedings for infringement of the patent. Kay found himself involved in many law-suits, and although he gained his cases in the courts, he was almost ruined by the expenses of prosecuting his claims. He was back in Bury in 1745, and in that year, along with Joseph Stell of Keighley, he obtained a patent (No. 612), for a small-ware loom, to be actuated by mechanical power instead of by hand. But this power-loom was never perfected, consequent upon his financial embarrassments and the opposition of the operatives. In the year 1753 a Bury mob broke into Kay's house, destroying everything they found, and he barely escaped with his life. Among his other inventions was a machine for making wire cards, and the original model is now exhibited in the South Kensington Museum.

In his *History of Manchester*, 1793, Dr. Aiken says :

" The cotton manufacture, originally brought from Bolton, is here carried on very extensively in most of its branches. A great number of factories are erected upon the rivers and upon

many brooks within the Parish (of Bury), for carding and spinning both cotton and sheep's wool, also for fulling woollen cloth.
The inventions and improvements here in different branches are
astonishing. One of the most remarkable is a machine made by
Mr. Robert Kay, son of the late Mr. John Kay, inventor of the
wheel or flying-shuttle, for making several cards at once to card
cotton or wool. The engine straightens wire out of the ring,
cuts it in lengths, staples it, crooks it into teeth, pricks the holes
in the leather, puts the teeth in, row after row, till the cards are
finished; all which it does at one operation of the machine, in
an easy and expeditious manner, by a person turning a shaft,
and touching neither the wire nor leather."

The people of Bury in 1753 little thought of the future of
their town. Yorkshire folk were as ready to take up the card-
setter as they had been to take to the flying-shuttle. Halifax,
Cleckheaton, and Brighouse were not slow in developing a trade
by the use of the "New Bendigo," as they vulgarly named this
wonderful little machine, not much larger than a present-day
sewing machine. Candid friends are often unwelcome advisers.
But I will venture to offer this bit of advice: If ever it should
happen a rising genius brings out or starts a good thing in Bury,
think twice before you drive it away. The object lesson at
Butcher Lane, compared with the Accrington offshoot at Castleton, in machine-making, suggests what might have been. And
in the Kays' experience, wire-drawing and card-making might
have been two of the great trades in Bury (as they have continued to this day in Halifax and neighbourhood) if bygone Bury
folk had been wider awake. In 1780 there was published in
London, by a writer who signed himself with only a " T.," *Letters
on the Utility and Policy of employing Machines to Shorten
Labour*. In this work a letter is quoted from John Kay, to the
Society of Arts, dated 1764, saying:

"I have a great many more inventions than what I have given in, and the reason I have not put them forward is the bad treatment that I have had from woollen and cotton factories in different parts of England twenty years ago, and then I applied to Parliament, and they would not assist me in my affairs, which obliged me to go abroad to get money to pay my debts and support my family."

There is the plaint of a broken-spirited man in this quotation. No notice of the above is found in the minutes of the Society of Arts. However, there is mention in the minutes of the Society for 1764 that a letter was received from Robert Kay with reference to his father's wheel-shuttle. After some inquiry, the secretary was instructed on 4th December, 1764, "to acquaint Mr. Kay that the Society does not know any person who understands the manner of using his shuttle." The Society of Arts were, by the showing of their secretary, almost as ignorant as the Bury mob of eleven years earlier. The Society of Arts, in London, in 1764, could not find anyone in England who could explain to them the manner of using the wheel-shuttle!

According to the author of the last-quoted work, John Kay "sought refuge in France, where he commenced business with the spinning machines smuggled out of England from Lancashire by one Holker some years before; and he is said to have died in France in obscurity and poverty." Surely the awakened love of Art in Bury will ere long redeem from oblivion the name of John Kay! In this matter Bury should not be behind Manchester when the Art Gallery is erected and adorned. Manchester, in her new Town Hall, thought it well to associate itself with this remarkable genius by commissioning Madox Brown to make John Kay and his fly-shuttle the subject for one of the frescoes for which the City Palace in Albert Square is now famous. The original portrait of John Kay is at the South Kensington Museum.

E

It has been lithographed, and has also been engraved by T. O.
Barlow as one of the series of portraits of inventors of textile
machinery, published by Messrs. Agnew in 1862. The Bury Art
Gallery ought to contain either the original, or as faithful a copy
of it as can be obtained. And by means of scholarships (if not
by a monument) the genius of John and Robert Kay ought to
be recognised in the town with which they were so intimately
identified, and whose inventions in connection with weaving—
improvements which are to-day indispensable—enable hundreds
of thousands of people to earn their livelihood.

NOTE.—The "fuller account" above is a paraphrase of the article on
JOHN KAY in *National Biography*, and like other accounts referred to is
qualified in many points of detail in the Memorial volume by the present
author entitled : *Memoir of John Kay, Inventor of the Fly-Shuttle.* Suffice
it here to remark that the inventor's father never had a works at Colchester,
and died in the month of April preceding the birth of his son, the inventor,
in July, 1704.

The authorities at South Kensington have informed the author that the
portrait of JOHN KAY there, belongs to the widow of the late Mr.
Bennett Woodcroft, and evidence has been found that it is an enlarged
copy of one at the Art Gallery in Bury.

BYGONE BURY.

CHAPTER V.

From the *Bury Times*, September 11th, 1897.

I PASS on to another family of Kays—William Kay and Company of Woolfold. This William Kay carried on for many
years a prosperous trade. Offshoots of sons, and prominent
men, were also helpful in carrying on the works of cotton
spinning and manufacturing, &c., elsewhere. James Duckworth,
one of the leading hands at Woolfold, became manager for the
Bury and Heap Commercial Company when this company commenced working at Chesham Field, Freetown. John Duckworth,
the son of this James, was a town salesman for Grundy, Kay, and
Co., Mosley Street, Manchester; and this firm were selected as
Manchester agents for the sale of yarns and cloth produced by
the Bury and Heap Commercial Company. The Kays in this
Manchester agency were two or three brothers, sons of the
William Kay of Woolfold. I recall the sons of this William Kay
in the persons of William—tall and somewhat ruddy featured—
Robert, James, and Hilton Kay. These four sons were not all
partners in the Manchester agency, so far as I know. James,
the third-named, seemed to me in those days the principal in the
firm. Associated with him, more or less actively, were Robert
and Hilton. And if my memory is accurate, this family or

branch of the Kays was formerly concerned in cotton spinning at the old mill in Heywood, near Wrigley Brook, which was, about the time I am writing of, in the occupation of the Mellors.

The Grundy family above referred to were John Grundy's sons, of Wolstenholme Hall, Bagslate. Two sons of this John Grundy were connected with the firm of Grundy, Kay, and Co. Their father had long been connected with the firm of Rothwell and Grundy, Limefield. He was son of the John Grundy, of Silver Street, Bury, who was brother of Edmund Grundy, of the Wylde, and of Elizabeth, of Seedfield. This lady will be remembered as "Miss Grundy," the devoted attendant at the Presbyterian Chapel, Bank Street, Bury. She and her brother Edmund for many years were teachers, and took a life-long interest in the Sunday School connected with Bank Street Chapel, particularly during the ministry of the Rev. Franklin Howorth. The John Grundy first-named (born 1810) at one period resided at The Dales, near Stand, Whitefield. He removed thence to Wolstenholme Hall as stated. " Grundy," says the author of a volume I have consulted, " is apparently the old Teutonic name Grund—whence Grundisborough, a parish in Suffolk." Wolstenholme (Hall) is the hall near the wolf stone, in the ancient wilds of Bagslate moor or common. And I may here show how in old deeds this is made more evident. In the days before the spelling reform was made general, even legal documents varied in the spelling of the same personal or place-names. In a very old surrender loaned to the present writer by the survivor of the elder branch of our family, I discover the origin of the word, and the early establishment of the old family residence ; also I find that the same locality gave a name to one of the families of bygone Bury. I will here set out the old deed, following the spelling, as therein given :

" Manor of Rachdale : The Copyhold Court of the Right honourable William, Lord Byron, Baron Rachdale, for govern-

ing and ordering of his Customary Lands within the Manor of
Rachdale in the County of Lancaster holden att Rachdale aforesaid the twenty-fourth day of December in the ninth year of the
Reign of our Sovereign Lord George the Second Over Great
Britain ffrance and Ireland King Defender of the ffaith and so
forth and in the year of our Lord One thousand seven hundred
and thirty-five. Before Robert Lownde Gentleman Steward of
the said Court and adjourned to the second day of ffebruary then
next ensueing and from thence to the fifth day of Aprill then
next ensueing before the same Steward afores^d Att this Court
It was found by the homase aforesaid that Joseph Wolstanholme
Late of Bury in the County of Lancaster Sadler a Customary
Tenant of this Manor dyed about eight weeks ago Seized of
and in One Messuage One Barn One Garden and two Acres of
Customary Land according to Eight yards to the Rood or Perch
Improved from the Soil or Waste of the said Manor called
Bagslate in Spotland within the said Manor and now or late in
the possession of John Leach his assigns or undertenants with
all ways waters and watercourses to the same belonging and that
Joseph Wolstenholme of Bury aforesaid Draper of the age of
fifty-three years or thereabouts is Eldest son and heir of the
said Joseph Wolstenholme deceased and ought to be admitted
to the said Customary Lands. And hereupon came into this
Court the said Joseph Wolstanholme (the son) in his own proper
person and craved to be admitted to his ffine. Upon proclama-
tion being made thereof and that if any man could pretend or
had any Right or Title to the aforesaid Copyhold Lands he might
come into Court and be heard And none came to forbid Then
seizing of the aforesaid Copyhold premises the Lord of the said
Manor by his Steward aforesaid did grant unto the said Joseph
Wolstanholme (the son) by a Rod according to the Custom of
the said Manor To have and to hold to him the said Joseph
Wolstanholme (the son) his heirs and assigns for Ever according

ffine for Entry 4d.

to the Custome of the said Manour Yeilding and paying therefor to the Lord of the said Manour of Current English att every feast of Saint Giles the Abbott and all other rents reliefs fines boons ectaments suits services and perquisites of Court which are or att any time hereafter shall become due and of right accustomed according to the Custom of the Manour aforesaid and he giveth to the Lord for a ffine entrance thereunto to be had and so forth by his pledge John Bury and is admitted Tenant thereof and hath done his ffealty.

A true Copy examined by

19th April 1737.   E. E. LOUNDES, STEWARD.

Here we have the fact made plain that the old residence at Wolf-stone was reclaimed from the wild moorland of Spotland. Harland in his *History of Lancashire,* vol. i., page 512, says that the ancient family of Wolstenholme claimed to be of Saxon descent. Andrew de Wolstenholme was living here in 1180. Holme means house. Wolf-stone may have been a large stone marking the spot where a wolf had been killed. Wolstenholme therefore would mean the house or residence near the Wolf-stone. Andrew would be all the name this ancient personage would have had given to him, but to distinguish him from other men of similar name he would be described as " Andrew de Wolstenholme "—Andrew of Wolf-stone-house. I imagine I am correct in my inference that the deed I have set out refers to Wolstenholme Hall of modern times. The John Grundy referred to as residing there died on the 23rd July, 1873, aged 63 years ; and I have an entry, probably copied from a funeral card, which reads thus :—" John Grundy, of Wolstenholme Hall, near Bircle, near Bury."

In my last paper I gave some information about John Kay, of Park, Walmersley. His inventions of the fly-shuttle, &c., lead

us to recall his successors in Bury. I have previously mentioned
" Jimmy " Shepherd of Mosses, whose mother was Ellen Kay of
" Cobbas," or Cobhouse, a daughter of Robert Kay. There is
no question whatever about this family connection, for Miss
Lucy Shepherd, a niece of this James Shepherd, yet residing in
Bury, recalls her grandmother distinctly, having in her youth
nursed her grandmother, Ellen Kay. And that she, Ellen, was
of the " Cobbas " family, cannot be in doubt, because she always
maintained that failing male heirs there was no doubt " all the
brass " would come to her grandchildren. The present writer,
being a great-grandchild, may be pardoned a slight sensation of
regret that " the brass " went elsewhere. But " brass " is not
always " wealth." It is useful to go an errand with, but its
absorbing influence over the mind often leads to the stunting
growth of the higher nature. Moralising, however, is not my
purpose here.

Among the bygones of Bury, in the present connection, I
may mention, as close to the period following the invention of
the fly-shuttle, Isaac Wood and Sons, shuttle makers, Back King
Street, Bury. Forty-eight years ago I knew this workshop.
The last of this old firm was a late townsman, John Wood,
of Clay Bank. He married Rachel, the daughter of Samuel
Wild, clerk to the Presbyterian Chapel, Bury. Sarah, the
younger sister of Mrs. John Wood, will be recalled as having
married William Grundy, son of Edmund Grundy, of the firm of
John and Edmund Grundy, of The Shed, Heap Bridge. Sup-
posing the fly-shuttle became popular about the time of the
events recorded previously, Isaac Wood and Sons would be
among the very earliest firms of shuttle makers in Lancashire.
The firm was not in being in 1818, but a few years later I find
" Isaac Wood, temple comb maker, King Street;" and no doubt
as his sons grew up, this Isaac Wood would add to his business

of temple combs the kindred one of shuttle making. However,
in 1824-5 he was temple-comb maker only.   There was in 1818
a John Wood, woollen manufacturer and shopkeeper, Moorside,
who is also recorded in 1824-5 contemporary with the firm of
William Walker and Sons, Stanley Street.   There was one shuttle
maker named in an earlier paper—" Thomas Butterfield, shuttle
maker, near Stanley Street," in 1818; who also appears again,
in 1825-6, as of 22, Fleet Street, Bury.   He would probably be
the son of Henry Butterfield and his wife, Mary Openshaw (she
was born in 1732), the daughter of John Openshaw and his wife,
Elizabeth Ormerod.   If I am correct in my inference, then this
Thomas Butterfield would receive the patronage of most of the
family connections engaged in weaving " cottons," and other
fabrics in Bury and district.   It is conceivable that Thomas
Butterfield would have youths apprenticed to his shuttle making
business, and that " Jimmy " Shepherd, of Mosses, and the sons
of Isaac Wood, would be among these early pupils.   It would be
about 1760-5 when Thomas Butterfield arrived at man's estate.
This was the era of Kay's invention.   About 1800 the appren-
tices would be also adepts at their trade.

The interval to bridge over, from 1800 to 1818 or 1825, is
not a long stretch for the imagination to attempt, and we find
ourselves then with power-looms recognised as of more importance
to the working classes of Lancashire than to be broken up,
except to make room for improved construction.   This reflection
leads on my thoughts to such a period of smashing up!   The
overpick-loom, at any rate for heavier fustian cloth, was found
unsuitable, and a time came when a man of the temperament of
John Lomax of Springfield, lost patience with the old-fashioned
machinery.   This impatience was the cause and opportunity of
mutual gratification and the development of another large firm
in Bury.   And that was a memorable day on which the indomit-

able John Lomax came down to the works, took out his snuff box for a good pinch as usual before giving expression to an important utterance, and said: " Go tell Robert Hall I want him at once." The messenger had instantly to hurry off to " Tuer, Hodgson, and Hall," the early firm established in Back King Street. Robert Hall was not slow to heed the summons. He probably returned more buoyant in spirit, for he took an order back for 400 new under-pick looms for No. 3 shed of the Moorside Works. I suppose it is not venturing too sanguine a statement if I say this was one source of the subsequent successes attained by the eminent firm now existing. After No. 3 came No. 4 shed, and so on all through the sheds, where ultimately about 1,400 looms of the new description were as speedily as possible got to work. It appeared to the youthful mind a sad destruction of good machinery to witness the old looms smashed up by sledge hammer, to be carted down and re-melted for moulding into new designs. But money was seen at the end of the conversion, I suppose. At any rate, it no doubt came. And our friends the shuttle makers and temple-comb makers had their busy time consequent upon the enterprise referred to, which doubtless was emulated by Charles Openshaw and Sons, Butcher Lane, Johnathan Openshaw of Elton, and the cotton side of the Pimhole Openshaws, all engaged in the heavier class of cotton manufactures, as distinguished from the ordinary calicoes of Burnley and Blackburn districts. So young readers may see something of how Bury, of the past, became prosperous; and elder readers may recall their share in the accomplishment of that prosperity.

Mention should also be made of another branch of the Kay family which became noted, and made a name outside Bury, also in mechanics. William Kay, of Bolton Street, in the matter of throstle spinning machinery was esteemed all over Lancashire.

Latterly this was carried on by his son, James Clarkson Kay, who undertook heavier work, in the way of increasing the expansive power of steam by means of a patent arrangement of valves and the patent brought out by McNaught. This caused another firm in Bury, the Brothers Lord, boiler makers, at Barnbrook, to become busy and prosperous, by reason of natural demand for boilers of great resistance to work at higher pressure. And here again we find the John Lomax, before-named, determined upon having the best boilers and engines. The boilers he ordered from the Barnbrook firm; the McNaughting of the engines was done elsewhere, and the changes were wrought in due course. There was a cylinder under each end of the beam; the smaller cylinder, placed next the crank because of limited space, took in the steam at the highest practicable pressure, and then exhausted into the old larger cylinder, from whence it found escape into the cold-water condenser. The pressure of the steam on the two pistons, added to the vacuum pressure of the atmosphere, obtained by the most efficacious air-pump and the coldest obtainable supply of water, secured the greatest possible power out of the water evaporated into steam by the smallest contrivable supply of coal. And this was how the trade of Bury became prosperous. Boilers from Barnbrook; engines from Butcher Lane; carding, slubbing, and other frames, and mules from Butcher Lane; throstles from Bolton Street; and looms from Back King Street or Heywood—yes, this was how the money was made in the bygone days of Bury.

NOTE.—The Isaac Wood mentioned in this chapter never was put apprentice to the Shuttle trade.

Mr. James Shepherd learned his trade as Shuttlemaker with the firm of Butterfield, relatives of the Openshaws of Pimhole. For a length of time he carried on the business of Machine making in Bolton Street, in partnership with his cousin, John Kay, of Cobhouse descent. Further reference will be made to him subsequently.

BYGONE BURY.

CHAPTER VI.

From the *Bury Times*, June 4th, 1898.

A WRITER IN 1818 states that there was a Charity School, for the education of 80 boys and 30 girls, founded by the late Rev. John Stanley, formerly Rector of Bury. I assume this would be what, in my younger days, was commonly called "Th' Free School," standing at the corner of Clough Street. I suppose the funds which the Rev. John Stanley left for the founding of this school are used for supporting some newer institution. The same writer just quoted goes on to say : " A variety of alterations and improvements are now (1818) making in the streets, which will add very much to the convenience and general appearance of the town." Many improvements have been effected since then, and those changes that the writer in question refers to have served their turn, and many of them have given place to still more stately edifices. The same writer says : " The cotton manufacture, originally brought from Bolton, is here carried on in all its various branches to a great extent. The whole parish abounds with factories, every convenient situation upon the rivers and brooks being occupied by mills for carding and spinning of wool and cotton ; and also for fulling woollen

cloth." Leland says: "Yerne sometime made about it—Byri "
in his day. These "yernes" might be of woollen or cotton
material. Previously to what is now understood as "cotton,"
the fabrics taken into the markets round about Bury, and to
Manchester, were named "cottons," even when manufactured of
wool.

As trade increased the population grew in numbers; and
Bury people wakened up to the fact that it was desirable and
expedient that a local government should be set up. Hitherto,
it may be supposed, little more had sufficed than the government
by the Vestry and Courts Leet of the Manors of Tottington and
Bury. I recollect as representative of the keeper of the peace
" Th' Owd Deputy," James Andrews. That the people were not
of a very turbulent type we may infer from the fact that the first
Petty Sessions held in Bury sat on 21st March, 1826. The first
magistrate was William Grant, appointed 1824, died 1842.
Samuel Holker Haslam was the next appointment, in 1829. He
died in 1856. These persons would know most about the
circumstances of the populations in the localities between Ramsbottom and Bury, either by way of Walmersley, or down the
valley to Bury Ground. In 1833 John Fenton appeared on the
Bench, representative of the district round by Ashworth, Crimble,
and Heywood. And in a little while we see more assistance
required; which was found by the appointment of Edmund
Grundy, who would know as much as anyone of the locality
about Heap Bridge. Seven years after this we find John Grundy
qualifying for Justice of the Peace. Perhaps he combined super-
vision over The Dales and Whitefield, as well as Limefield. This
John Grundy I assume to have been co-partner in the firm of
Rothwell and Grundy, of Limefield, or it may have been his
father. The following year, 1842, Henry Hardman took his
seat on the Bench; and three years after William Hutchinson.

On July 27th, 1846, an Act of Parliament was granted establishing a commission, for the government of Bury. The name given to this authority was "The Bury Improvement Commission." I do not profess special knowledge of the early formation of this Commission, but I am old enough to recall my impressions of many of the first Commissioners elected, and have made an alphabetical list of all the 120 who were elected Commissioners during the thirty years of the existence of this Board.

The first election took place in 1846, and the last in 1876. Of those elected in 1846, Micah Barlow sat one year, William Barrett three years, William Bowman four years, Henry Bridge four years, William Bridge one year, Christopher Clemishaw thirteen years, John Clemishaw three years, Matthew Fletcher eight years, Thomas Greenhalgh, jun. four years, Edmund Hardman three years, John Hoyle the elder three years, John Haslam one year, Thomas Horrocks eleven years, John Lomax three years, John Mitchell fourteen years, Thomas Openshaw five years, Thomas Oram two years, Oliver Ormerod Openshaw three years, John Openshaw seven years, Jonathan Openshaw five years, Lawrence Rogers Openshaw two years, Lawrence Park six years, James Parks twelve years, Matthew Peel twenty-five years, John Rothwell four years, Robert Taylor four years, and Richard Walker, jun. fifteen years. Here we have an exemplification of the old saying : " The last shall be first." Richard Walker, jun., was the first Chairman of the Board of Commissioners, 1846-7, and again 1851-2, 1856-7, 1857-8, 1863-4, and 1864-5. In fact for ten out of the fifteen years that he sat as Commissioner he was deservedly the Chairman. We have noteworthy evidence of the great interest taken in the management of the town's affairs by that generation of rising capitalists and great employers of labour in Bury.

I am indebted to a somewhat pretentious Bury history for the

foregoing list of names, but have difficulty in correctly supplying
the descriptions of some of the persons named. Probably some
of my readers will be able to correct mistakes. I will only identify these first Improvement Commissioners tentatively, by asking
if it was not the case that Micah Barlow was the father of
Thomas and John Barlow of Barlow Fold, Manchester Road, or
was he an elder brother of Thomas and John, and all of them
sons of " Frances Barlow, grocer, &c., Redevals ;" or, " James
Barlow, victualler and hatter, White Bear, Wilde ? " Then was
William Barrett the William Barrett (Baines gives it Barritt),
butcher, at one time of 17, Fleet Street? In one record the
name is spelt Barratt, in other cases Barrett. " John Clemishaw,
joiner and shopkeeper, Henry Street "—would he be identical
with the Commissioner? And would Christopher be his son or
brother, and, if brother, both be sons of " David Clemishaw,
builder, of Paradise Street ? " William Bowman, chemist and
druggist, was well known in his day. Henry Bridge—was he not
a draper? William Bridge I recall as a draper, if not his
brother. Matthew Fletcher, I assume, was the venerable surgeon, who resided previously at 59, Union Square. Thomas
Greenhalgh, jun., would doubtless be the " Cotton Spinner,
Chesham." In 1825 his house was in " Clark Street." Edmund
Hardman I cannot trace, unless he was the son of William Hardman, of Chamber Hall. John Haslam was presumably representative of the firm " Haslam and Son, Hudcarr Works." In
Thomas Horrocks I identify the person of that name who resided
in Wike's Lane. But in 1825 and 1826 there was a Thomas
Horrocks residing at " 14, Clerke Street." Readers will note
the varying spelling; one writer gives " Clark Street," another
" Clerke Street." Probably the street was named after a former
rector—Sir William Henry Clerke. John Lomax was our acquaintance of Springfield. In the Rent Roll of Sir John Pilkington, of Bury, *tempo* 1435, his name is spelt " del Lumhalghes."

In 1600-1620, it was spelt " Lummas ; " and it was not till 1663 that it was written " Lomax." John Mitchell I can clearly identify. He was waste buyer for James Wrigley and Sons, Bridge Hall Paper Mills ; as well as head of the old firm of Mitchell and Co., Spindle Works, Bury. He was a man of fine physique, and a good public speaker. Earlier or later he was associated with Clitheroe. The Thomas Openshaw who sat for five years was, I believe, the " Mr. Thomas," of Primrose Hill, Pimhole. His cousin Thomas, of High Bank, was not a Commissioner at any time, if my impression is correct. And the third Thomas Openshaw, living at this period, nephew of Thomas of High Bank, would be engaged under John Walker at the mill in Elton. Thomas Oram might be the gentleman recorded as of " 43, Fleet Street," in my record. He would be father of Henry Oram of a later period. Oliver Ormerod Openshaw is unquestionably our old acquaintance in these notes, of Roach Bank, Pimhole. Then John Openshaw, the name following— I can only surmise that he was of Irwell House, often described as " Long John," because of his stature. Jonathan Openshaw I incline to think identical with " Little Jonathan ; " but there was another Jonathan. Lawrence Rogers Openshaw would be our " famous horseman " of Brickhouse. And Lawrence Park I know must be the " burly-boniface " of the Old White Horse, who also was carrier to the East Lancashire Railway Company. James Parks, of 1846 Board, I put down to be James Parks, surgeon ; though the connection of James Park, ironfounder, with the Board suggests the possibility of correction. In Matthew Peel we have the stalwart currier of Bury Tanpits. His brother Henry was an ironmonger at the premises afterwards so marvellously developed by my late old friend, Joseph Downham. John Rothwell, I surmise, was the cotton manufacturer of Limefield. Robert Taylor I am not clear about ; he may have been

the person of that name who in 1825-6 was "cotton manufacturer at Moorside." Richard Walker requires no identifica-
tion beyond the statement that he was the eldest son of Bury's
first Member of Parliament, and in every respect worthy to pre-
side over the first local governing body of his native town. On
the first Board of Commissioners were the largest ratepayers,
the keenest business men of the town; and in this fact was the
assurance that the improvements would be judiciously inaugu-
rated and economically carried forward.

In the interval between 1846 and 1876 one generation passed
away and another rose up, and the Commissioners who succeeded
the aforementioned were men of considerable standing in the
town. The system adopted in the election of the Commissioners
was calculated to rouse the latent enthusiasm of the populace.
Party feeling then was shown in the discrimination of Church
and Chapel proclivities. "Exclusive dealing" sometimes was
fostered. "Local influence" was brought to bear; for then
there was no voting by ballot. But even as passions were
excited and influence exerted to secure the election of certain
nominees, it was more the question of Church or Chapel than
actual fitness or unfitness of the candidates. However, a survey
of the several Boards during the thirty years existence of the Bury
Improvement Commissioners will convince the impartial reader
that "good men and true" were ever to be found. The names
of the other Commissioners are appended in alphabetical order,
with the year they first were elected, and the number of years
they sat; also indicating, where I can do so, the religious
distinctions :

Alcock John (Bank Street), 1852, 1 year; Hudcar.
Alcock R. H. (Bank Street), 1856, 5 years; Hudcar.
Aitkin Thomas, 1853, 2 years.
Ashworth Abel (Wesleyan), 1866, 4 years; Rochdale Road.

Ashworth Adam (Wesleyan), 1867, 6 years ; Pits-o'-th'-Moor.

Barlow Edward, 1860, 10 years.

Barlow Thomas (Church), 1869, 4 years.

Barrett James (Church), 1849, 9 years ; Pimhole.

Barrett John (Church), 1861, 3 years ; (?) Pimhole.

Battersby Robert, junr. (Church), 1847, 4 years ; Parsons Lane.

Bate Edward (Bank Street), 1855, 1 year ; boot and shoe maker.

Booth Geoge (Bank Street), 1861, 6 years ; at Walker Brothers, and then pawnbroker.

Bolton John, 1868, 5 years ; brother-in-law to William Fairbrother

Blunt Thomas, 1872, 1 year ; waste dealer, formerly cashier for James Wrigley and Sons, Bridge Hall Mills.

Booth Lawrence, 1871, 2 years ; architect.

Clemishaw Joseph, 1850, 3 years ; druggist ; Moorside.

Cook Samuel, 1864, 8 years ; reedmaker.

Crossland Robert, 1866, 6 years ; solicitor.

Crompton W. R., 1871, 2 years ; papermaker.

Davenport William (Church), 1855, 3 years ; tinner.

Duckworth John (Bank Street), 1870, 3 years ; bleacher.

Davies Thomas Clifford, 1872, 1 year ; surgeon ; Rhiwlas.

Fletcher Thomas, 1860, 8 years ; (?) chemist.

Fairbrother William, 1867, 6 years ; Chairman of the Crimble Spinning Company.

Grundy Samuel (Bank Street), 1852, 1 year ; (?) Bridge Hall.

Grundy Thomas (Bank Street), 1852, 11 years ; solicitor, T. A. and J. G.

Grundy William (Bank Street), 1856, 1 year ; Seedfield.

Grundy Edward Herbert (Bank Street), 1868, 2 years ; Bridge Hall and Cheetham Hill.

Harper William (Roman Catholic), 1848, 10 years ; solicitor.

Haworth George, 1849, 3 years ; Plumtrees ; formerly of Simpson, Bland, and Haworth.

Hoyle James (Church), 1848, 6 years; cotton spinner, Huntley Brook.

Hoyle John (Church), 1852, 8 years; (?) John and Samuel Hoyle, Ferngrove.

Holt John (Bank Street), 1850, 19 years; tailor.

Hall Robert (Brunswick), 1850, 19 years; of Tuer, Hodgson, and Hall.

Hutchinson John (Church), 1853, 3 years; Colonel of the Volunteers.

Haworth Richard, 1853, 4 years; son of George above.

Hacking Richard, 1860, 2 years; " Dick," of Walker and Hacking.

Hamer John, 1860, 4 years; bookkeeper to Walker and Lomax.

Hill James (Bank Street), 1864, 1 year; stone merchant; son-in-law of Thomas Hopkinson.

Holt Thomas, 1860, 9 years; druggist; Bolton Street; Chairman of Bury and Heap Commercial Company.

Horrocks John (Bank Street), 1863, 3 years; of the Albion Hotel.

Kenyon William, 1868, 1 year; probably of the firm of drapers and undertakers.

Kay James, 1849, 12 years; of the Blue Bell, Barnbrook.

Kay James Clarkson (Wesleyan), 1849, 4 years; ironfounder and engineer.

Kay Robert, 1868, 2 years; for a generation with Thomas, Alfred, and John Grundy.

Kenyon Richard, 1857, 2 years.

Kershaw Jacob, junr., 1858, 2 years; Pimhole.

Livesey James, 1851, 3 years; Bank Street and Heap Bridge.

Mitchell Thomas, 1860, 5 years; brother of John, a first Commissioner.

Maxwell James (Wesleyan), 1871, 2 years; caddy sheet manufacturer.

Newbold Joseph, 1857, 10 years; The Springs.

Nuttall John, 1863, 6 years; probably the corn dealer.

Openshaw James, 1847, 8 years; whether of Redvales or Fernhill, not sure.

Openshaw George (St. John's), 1855, 8 years; Heywood Street.

Oram Henry, 1858, 1 year; brief, but remembered.

Openshaw Samuel, 1859, 3 years; Red Lion.

Openshaw Thomas, 1860, 12 years; of John Walker's and then of Brickhouse.

Openshaw Thomas Lomax, 1854, 3 years; well-known son of " Little Jonathan."

Openshaw James Alfred, 1869, 3 years; eldest son of James Openshaw, of Beech Hill, Pimhole.

Ormerod Thomas, 1872, 1 year.

Pilkington Joseph, 1847, 1 year; woollen manufacturer.

Pilkington John, 1848, 2 years; woollen manufacturer.

Pilkington James, 1850, 1 year; woollen manufacturer.

Peel Henry, 1854, 12 years; brother to Matthew, and predecessor of Joseph Downham, ironmonger.

Pickering John, 1849, 6 years; brushmaker, Bolton Street.

Park James, 1850, 20 years; father of the Bury waterworks, I am inclined to think.

Potts Edward, 1850, 1 year; draper, Bolton Street.

Price Thomas, junr., 1852, 4 years.

Price William, 1857, 2 years.

Price, W. H., 1858, 1 year.

Price Thomas Lloyd, 1860, 1 year.

Parker James, 1862, 1 year; currier, Stanley Street.

Polding Peter Oswald, 1851, 1 year; veterinary surgeon.

Peers Robert, 1867, 6 years; pawnbroker, Bolton Street.

Parkinson John, 1854, 17 years; brassfounder, Mosses.

Roberts Thomas, 1854, 15 years; Chesham Fields.

Renshaw Samuel, 1861, 9 years; cotton manufacturer, Freetown.

Rothwell Samuel, 1858, 2 years.

Smith Daniel, 1849, 3 years; corn merchant.

Smith Samuel (Brunswick), 1859, 8 years; woollen manufacturer, King Street.

Sykes Joseph, 1868, 5 years; Freetown.

Unwin John, 1854, 5 years; spirit merchant.

Unsworth James, 1871, 2 years; of Goshen Farm.

Walker John Scholes, 1855, 7 years; of the Butcher Lane firm.

Wood Robert, 1850, 21 years, Rochdale Road; father-in-law of Thomas Openshaw of Brickhouse.

Whitehead James, 1851, 3 years; tailor; brother of "gentleman" Samuel Whitehead, tailor.

Wanklyn William, jun., 1854, 6 years; cotton spinner, Elton; brother-in-law of Colonel O. O. Walker.

Webb Joseph, 1856, 16 years; of the Forge, Bury Bridge.

Wormald John, 1867, 5 years; dentist, Bank Street.

Ward Richard, 1860, 8 years; of Butcher Lane Works; built Bradford Terrace.

Wike John Melling, 1860, 3 years; son of George Wike, and eminent in music and Masonry.

Walker Charles, 1869, 3 years; (?) son of Richard of Belle Vue.

Young John, jun., 1853, 3 years; Savings' Bank.

There is no pretension to originality in giving the foregoing names of persons who served their town in their day and generation, but the mere enumeration will recall to many readers pleasant associations of "Bygone Bury."

BYGONE BURY.

CHAPTER VII.

From the *Bury Times*, June 11th, 1898.

THERE are names in the foregoing chapters which suggest still earlier firms than those already mentioned, whose descendants are still found in Bury. For example, Blomley Bothers, 1818, fulling millers, Bridge Hall, are no doubt the same family of which one member formerly resided in Clerke Street; Edmund Bolland, 1818, blacksmith, Heap Bridge (mentioned in the Openshaws of Beech Hill reminiscences); Edward Rothwell, 1818, gentleman, Spout Bank; William Rothwell, 1818, farmer, Spout Bank; Edmund Whitworth, 1818, farmer, Littlebridge; William Wild, farmer, Gigg; and somewhat further afield I find, at Crimble, John Kenyon, farmer. It may only be a coincidence as to name and locality that the Crimble Spinning Company, were, I believe, tenants of the father of the present Member of Parliament for Bury. In 1818 there was Charles Kenyon, woollen manufacturer, New Road; house, 41, Union Square. Would this be the founder of the present prosperous firm in Derby Street? Was the late James Clarkson Kay the son and successor of William Kay, ironfounder and nail manufacturer, 7, bottom of Bolton Street, in 1818? There was also a James Kay,

foundryman, Moorside. Was James Davenport, woollen manufacturer, 1818, Back-o'-th'-Square, or Peter Davenport, blacksmith and wheelwright, Redivals, father of William the tinsmith
in Water Street? The last-named married Mary Openshaw,
daughter of John Openshaw, of Pimhole and Rosehill, Bury;
and I believe a daughter of this William and his wife Mary
married Thomas Nuttall, architect. We find, in 1818, Joseph
Downham, joiner and cabinet maker, Tenterfield, and I surmise
he was the father of John Downham, sharebroker; Joseph Downham, lately deceased; and William Downham, watchmaker.
Many old Bury people will recall William Goodlad, surgeon, of
Bolton Street. Also the Old Eagle and Child, Silver Street,
kept by Elizabeth Handley—in 1818 passed to her son, James
Handley; the license being ultimately removed to the present
Derby Hotel. Joseph Handley, son of James Handley, became
manager of the Bury Banking Company, after William Coward.
There was a severe crisis at this epoch in the history of that bank
which necessitated the writing off of upwards of £100,000; and
yet Bury was not swamped. Vicissitudes in trade and commerce
seem to follow in cycles. You have had your wealthy Grundys,
Ashtons, and Openshaws; your representatives of hunting and
other sporting proclivities. We have named Matthew and Henry
Peel. The first of these succeeded his father, Henry Peel, who
in 1818 was carrying on leather tanning at the Tan Pits. Matthew
married Mary daughter of Samuel Kay, hatter, Wash Lane, and
his wife Mary the daughter of Robert Shepherd and his wife
Ellen Kay of Cobbas, and had a family; and on the death of
this wife Matthew Peel married her cousin, a daughter of Robert
Shepherd of Silver Street, and his wife Betty Nuttall. In 1818
there was a John Scholes, cotton manufacturer, 13, Stanley
Street; possibly Jacob Scholes, confectioner, Moorside, was a
kinsman of this John, but I cannot speak as to the connection

of this family with the Walker family. There was at this period a Samuel Smith, machinist, Butcher Lane, and it is probable that Walker and Hacking took over that business. I also find in 1818 John Wike, who married Margaret the daughter of George Openshaw of Seales, woollen manufacturer, house in New Road (what was called Wike Lane may here be meant); he would be followed in that trade by his son George Wike, the present Mayor being a younger son of the latter. And there was at the same period Samuel Woodcock, solicitor, Henry Street; and John Woodcock, surgeon, Church Yard. At a later period there was Samuel Woodcock, also solicitor, of Henry Street, succeeded by Samuel Woodcock, solicitor of to-day. In the order these Samuels appear I am inclined to designate them father, son, and nephew. The last-named I believe is a younger son of William Plant Woodcock, solicitor, and his wife Miss Yates, the square brick house at the top of New Road and Pimhole Lane, now utilised as a club, being some time their residence. The marriages of sons and daughters of James Openshaw, of Lower Chesham, and his wife Martha Ann, the daughter of John Jackson of Bury (the said James Openshaw being some time fourth partner in the firm of Walkers and Lomax), connected three old families of Bury. Hannah, the eldest daughter, married John Hoyle of Mossfield; Margaret, the second daughter, married Mr. S. Woodcock; James Henry Openshaw, as has been mentioned earlier, married Susannah, daughter of Joseph Newbold; while John Jackson Openshaw, the elder brother of this James Henry, married Emma, daughter of John Howard, co-founder of the great Accrington firm of Howard and Bullough, machinists. Two sons and two daughters of this James Openshaw and his wife Martha Ann died in infancy. Emma, the fifth daughter and eighth child, born 1853, married James Strang of the Peel, Busby, near Glasgow; and Fanny, the next child, married James Millership Stead, of Carr Bank, Ramsbottom.

In Bury and neighbourhood there has been for centuries the family of Nuttall. Old writings give the early name " Notogh." " Nuttall Hall, in the Hamlet of Holcombe and Township of Tottington, was the seat of Richard de Notogh, born before 1368 and living in 1397-1408; it descended to Richard de Notogh, living 1493-4." Ultimately this estate passed, probably by marriage, to the Lonsdale family; and from that family, in similar manner, to the Rev. Richard Formby, about 1790. By him it was sold to Mr. Grant (Harland). And I find another record of Harland : " John, son of Nicholas Golyn, of Golynrode in Walmersley in the Parish of Bury, conveyed Golynrode by deed, dated 7th September, 1491, to Henry Notogh of Notogh ; and the arms and crest allowed in 1664 to Thomas Nuttall, of Tottington, claiming to represent a collateral branch, were allowed by order of Chapter in 1841 to George Ormerod of Tyldesley and Sedbury, as heir general of Nuttall of Golynrode. In *Ducatus Lancastriæ* I find mention among the Pleadings, I. Eliz., 1559, of Ralph Gollyn, as Heir of John Gollyn, plaintiff ; George Nuthough and Roger Holte, defendants. The cause in dispute was " A Messuage, Lands, Tenements, and Hereditaments, Bury." This action in the Duchy Court of Lancaster, in the year 1559, two generations after the conveyance mentioned by Harland, would seem to be in reference to a small estate other than the mansion and land of Golynrode. We have in the two transactions the names of three generations of Gollyn—Nicholas Gollyn, probably of about 1400-1450 ; his son John, about 1450-1520 ; and Ralph, the " heir of John," 1559. We see the Ormerods connected with the Nuttalls. The aforementioned George Ormerod was an only child, at any rate the only son, of George Ormerod and his wife Anne, the daughter of

John Hutchinson of Bury, merchant; and this last-named George was brother of Elizabeth, the wife of John Openshaw of Pimhole, of Alice the wife of James Openshaw of Walmersley, and of Rachel the wife of Robert Booth of Bury, all these daughters and this son George being children of Oliver Ormerod of Bury and his wife Alice Howarth of Chatterton Hey, Tottington. So that we find Ormerod, Hutchinson, Openshaw, Howarth, and Booth all family names of bygone Bury. To refer once more to the Nuttall family : Robert Shepherd, weaver, Silver Street, Bury, married Ann Nuttall. This Robert Shepherd was son of Robert Shepherd and his wife Ellen Kay of " Cobbas." The Booth estate was sold to James Lomax of Unsworth, one of whose daughters married in 1693 John Halliwell of Pike House; and one of John Halliwell's descendants, John Beswicke, devised it by will, 1772, and it was bought in 1796 by Robert Nuttall, Bury. Bridge Hall was in 1482 the residence of Roger Holt (a younger son of Holt of Grislehurst), who married Jane, daughter of Thomas Greenhalgh of Brandlesome, who recorded a short pedigree. His son, Richard Holt, married Sarah, daughter of Robert Bellis, M.A., and was living 1706, having a daughter and heir who married Nathaniel Gaskell of Manchester. Were these Gaskells connected with the learned William Gaskell of Cross Street Chapel, Manchester, whose wife was so intimate with the Bröntes ? In 1736 Robert Nuttall bought the Bridge Hall estate, and his descendants sold it to Edmund Grundy. The following copy of an entry of a marriage at Radcliffe Parish Church in 1656 may not be without interest to the families whose names are mentioned :—" Thomas Openshaw, gent., son of John Openshaw, late of Radcliffe, deceased, and Sarah, daughter of Peter Walker, of the Parish of Prestwich, yeoman, both aged 21 and upwards, were married at Hopwood, 1656." (Radcliffe Register Book). It seems to me, if we may reason upon the way in which families in bygone Bury arranged their love affairs, that there is a probability that the Richard Walker of Stone Pale Farm, Whitefield, and his sister Margaret, were children's children of the above marriage. This Richard Walker married Rachel Grundy of Baldingstone, and his sister married Thomas Openshaw of Stanley Street.

NOTE.—In this chapter mention is made of George Ormerod of Tyldesley and Sedbury, as heir general of Nuttalls of Tottington. This George was the Historian of Cheshire. His *History of Cheshire* has recently been acquired by the Bury Corporation Library, and will be found in the Reference Department. Three immense volumes, in perfect condition, as new from the Press.

The Ann referred to in the present chapter was cousin to Dr. William Nuttall of Manchester Road, Bury, descendant of the Mr. Frank Nuttall, who in the period of the firm of Peel and Yates, at Bury Ground, held a good position there.

In the foregoing chapter mention is made of Mr. Samuel Kay, hatter, Wash Lane. It may come within the scope of these notes to point out his descent from the Kays who left Sheephey and purchased the Park Estate. His ancestry leads back through William Kay who farmed Snape Hill Farm, to Thomas Kay, born 1730, who claimed to be half-cousin to the inventor of the fly-shuttle.

The Chart published in the *Memoir of John Kay*, the inventor of the fly-shuttle, more clearly exemplifies this lineage. Samuel had a brother John Kay, grocer and flour dealer, who was always claimed as cousin by a descendant of William of Snape Hill. If so, we have the Kays of Park and Kays of Cobhouse united in the above wedding of Samuel Kay and Mary Shepherd.

The reference to a wedding at Radcliffe in 1656, mentioned in the last paragraph, lends some interest to the following note culled by the author in a recent visit to Knowsley Hall to examine, by permission, the old lease book there:—" 10th October 1688 lease for three lives to Mary Walker; the lives were Richard, son, aged 50; Thomas Hand, aged 21; James Meadowery, aged 17."

"7th August 1752 lease for three lives to Richard Walker; the lives were Peter Walker, grandson, aged 5; Tabitha Walker, granddaughter, aged 8; John, son of John Barber, aged 12."

BYGONE BURY.

NAMES AND PLACES.

CHAPTER VIII.

From the *Bury Times*, November 12th, 1898.

THE writer has been favoured by a lady well known to Bury people with permission to examine some old books of account and a large number of papers pertaining to the descendants of John Kay, inventor of the fly-shuttle. There may be some interest attaching to these long-buried and almost forgotten people and places. Robert Kay, inventor of the drop-box for looms, was the son of the afore-named John Kay. Robert Kay was survived by one son and two daughters. The son, Samuel Kay, resided at 44, Fleet Street, Bury, up to the date of his death, 28th December, 1830. Lucy Kay, the elder of the two daughters, married Thomas Oram, solicitor, Bury; and Dorothy, the younger daughter, married John Barlow, of Pump House, Antrobus, in the county of Chester. Robert Kay carried on a business in Bury almost to the end of his life; a fuller notice of him will be found in the *Memoir of John Kay* by the present author. Robert Kay was one of the executors and trustees under the will of James Fletcher, who died 21st February, 1780.

From February 23rd, 1780, to the end of Robert Kay's life in 1802, he was a most painstaking trustee of the estate left by James Fletcher, and the accounts kept by Robert Kay afford, as the writer thinks, many names and places the mention of which will be appreciated by local antiquaries:

May 3, 1780: Richd. Ormrod pays half-year's rent for Marshes estate; James Magnall pays half-year's rent for Brookbottom; Edward Fletcher pays half-year's rent for Little Millhouse; Ben. Buckley pays interest on a loan; John Rothwell pays half-year's rent for Woodroad; Jno. Holt pays part of half-year's rent for Nabbs estate.

May 16, 1780: Oliver Holden pays half-year's rent for Hill-end estate.

August 4, 1780: John Holt and James Spencer pay half-year's rent for Top of Royle estate.

August 5, 1780: John Moss pays cash for interest. Upon this date it would seem that the testator's library was put up to auction, and among the purchasers were Mr. Bevan, Mr. Nangreave, Mr. Walker (Oliver), and Samuel Fletcher.

December 26, 1780: Mr. Charles Hill pays a sum for interest.

February 5, 1781: Jere. Kay pays an interest account.

February 6, 1781: Jno. Nuttall pays a sum of money " for the late Robt. Kay's note."

February 17, 1781: Mr. Hargreaves pays rent for orchard.

February 19, 1781: Jno. Fletcher pays part of loan and interest, and Richd. Holt pays for some books.

February 20, 1781: Wm. Bentley receives cash from Mr. Ormrod to hand to Robt. Kay, the executor, for interest.

February 20, 1781: Mr. Beavan buys a house and part of the orchard from executors. And this date John and Thos. Ramsbottom (Harewood Fields) pay some interest. John Kay pays off a portion of principal. At this time John Booth, Thomas Haslam, Mr. Higgin, James Heaton, John Hargreaves, and Mr. Brandwood pay cash for goods, books, or interest.

May 3, 1781: Jere. Kay pays off money owing on bond with interest.

September 15, 1781 : John and Richd. Holt pay rent for Nabbs.

October 28, 1781 : Messrs. Taylor, Hargreaves, and Openshaw pay a sum of money for interest.

November 8, 1781 : Revd. John Smith and Jno. Nuttall pay off remainder due on " the late Robt. Kay of Park " bond. It would be interesting to know if such a co-partnership then existed as styled Taylor, Hargreaves, and Openshaw : and also to know if the Revd. Jno. Smith and Jno. Nuttall were executors of the Will of " the late Robt. Kay of Park."

November 20, 1781 : Messrs. Yates, Ryder, and Bridge pay off their bond. We find James Haydock, J. Fitton, Wm. Howard, and Thomas Hardman all paying interest at this time.

July 17, 1782 : Rich. Lomax pays some interest, and the previous day Thomas Haslam pays a very large sum as principal and interest. The aforenamed continue to pay interest upon money lent. Presumably many if not all of them were engaged in some sort of trade.

June 17, 1783 : Dionisius Hargreaves pays interest.

June 28, 1784 : Charles Holt and Jno. Spencer pay a sum of money in lieu of repairs wanting at Top of Royle.

December 19, 1785 : Booth Bridge pays a dividend upon a small sum owing the late Mr. Fletcher by John Bridge.

August 31, 1786 : John Butterworth pays on account of the late John Ramsbottom, interest.

April 8, 1787 : Thomas Wardle pays some interest on account of the late John Ramsbottom.

November 18, 1787 : Abram Wolfenden pays interest on account of the late John Ramsbottom. It would appear John Butterworth, Thomas Wardle, and Abram Wolfenden were executors " of the late John Ramsbottom's " Will.

November 30, 1787 : Mr. Nangreave pays interest upon a pretty large loan.

December 26, 1787 : Richd. Ramsbottom pays £4 4s. for a ring.

February 16, 1788 : Samuel Kay begins to pay interest.

November 17, 1788 : Jo. Wood and Mr. Norris pay account to executors " by a note from Mr. Robert Peel and Co. " which balances their (Wood and Norris's) account. This note is entered on credit side as an advance to " Mr. Robt. Peel and Co." on their note of £150.

April 29, 1789 : Mr. Robert Peel and Co. paid off their note and interest, £153 7s. 5d.—showing how in those days large firms obtained help from trust funds.

January 14, 1791 : Mr. Nangreave is still paying interest.

January 17, 1791 : Messrs. Ramsbottom pay executors by a bill drawn on Mr. Battersby. This shows the firm at Harwood Fields trading with the early generation of Battersbys of Bury.

In 1797 Mr. Milne is acting as executor of the late John Ramsbottom's Will.

December 6, 1799 : Mr. Nangreave pays off his loan.

December 20, 1800 : Messrs. Ramsbottom pay a bill drawn in favour of Mrs. Alice Fletcher — presumably the testator's widow.

September 6, 1801 : Thos. Haslam pays £3 14s. " for wood taken from Brookbottom."

August 19, 1802 : Thos. Rothwell pays £7 " for wood taken from Brookbottom."

These accounts close by a balance struck on the 4th December, 1802. Robert Kay died December 28, 1802, aged 76. The legatees under James Fletcher's Will were Alice Hargreaves, Betty Hargreaves, John Ramsbottom, Olive Ramsbottom, Saml. Ramsbottom, Margaret Bentley, Alice Bentley, Olive Bentley, Hannah Holt, Alice Pilkington, Ann Lomax, Andrew Lomax, Alice Heaton, Peter Hamer, Betty Hargreaves, and Joseph Page.

BYGONE BURY.

CHAPTER IX.

From the *Bury Times*, November 19th, 1898.

THOSE readers interested in the particulars given of Robert Kay's accounts of his executorship of James Fletcher's Will may have their interest increased by the knowledge that there is a gravestone, in the Parish Church of St. Mary, Bury, bearing the following particulars : — " Richard Fletcher, of Tottington, died 28th January, 1737, in his 54th year. Catherine Fletcher, his wife, died 8th January, 1767, in her 82nd year. James Fletcher, of Bury, gentleman, died 21st February, 1780, aged 63 years." There seems no doubt that this is the record of the death of the testators for whom Robert Kay, the inventor of the drop-box, was one of the executors, and probably of his parents. Changes are continually taking place in Bury, and places of historical interest are swept away, without apparent remorse. There may be among my readers some who are curious to know more about the inventor's family than the bare item that " John Kay was born at Park, near Bury, in 1704." If there are any amateur photographers in Bury, interested in this subject, I suggest they should lose no time in taking some views

of old premises in and around Bury. I will suggest one. Let
them wend their way to Moorside. There, numbers 18 and 20
will indicate the location of the old stone-built premises, once
occupied by " Cardmaker Kay," which premises were the object
of attack more than one hundred years ago of the blind, infatuated
mob, against which the soldiery were called out, and posted so
as to protect the Kays' works from utter destruction. These
premises are three storeys high. They are flanked by very old
brick-built houses ; and a perspective view of the whole range of
buildings, from the round house to the crossing street into
Badgers Fields, will form an interesting picture of a locality in
Bury which, a century ago, was the most significantly interesting
in the town ! Readers may fancy to themselves the operations
going on, in the upper chambers, of card-setting, and probably
fly-shuttle making. Some particulars about shuttles will be given
in a future chapter. Who, in Bury, got possession of the late
Mr. George Booth's wonderful collection of old shuttles ? However impoverished John Kay became, his son Robert appears to
have prospered.

Very old Bury people may recall the great changes made
round about the Old Market Place. If you could produce a
small map of Bury, as it was round about the Old Cross (the
site now occupied by the statue of Sir Robert Peel), you would
discover great changes made in Fleet Street and the Old Market
Place. Imagine a line brought from Agur Street, straight with
the front of the Athenæum, Town Hall, and part of the Derby
Hotel, and continued into Fleet Street, you would perceive that
a space would be open, which has been thrown into the street
from the present end of Fleet Street. Fleet Street houses and
premises in the olden time came up to the tall lamp which lights
the locality now. The present street arrangement and the Fleet
Street end of the Derby Hotel occupy the sites of property once

owned by John Kay's descendants. This property was included in a larger lease, and was purchased by the first Thomas Oram, attorney, Bury; and subsequently sold by him to his father-in-law, Robert Kay, son of John Kay, inventor of the fly-shuttle. When the lease fell in to Lord Derby the new Derby Hotel became possible. Mr. Oram's portion was occupied by the old Bull's Head and other premises. I will give some details of these tenancies in a future paper. At present some particulars of the above-mentioned lease will, no doubt, interest my readers :—

" Abstract of Indenture made 17th May the 37th George III., 1797, between Thomas Faulkner Phillips, Manchester, county Lancaster, Merchant, Richard Kay of Stand, within Pilkington of sd Cty Merchant and Benjamin Potter of Manchester aforesaid Merchant Devisces in fee and Executors of the Will of Joseph Baron late of Manchester aforesd Merchant decd of the One part and Thomas Oram of Bury in the sd Co. of the other part. Whereas by an Indenture of Lease 1782 made or mentioned to be made by Edward Earl of Derby on the One pt and said Joseph Baron of the other part for the consideration therein mentioned the sd Earl granted the Messuage or Dwelling house and Hereditaments hereinafter mentioned and intended to be hereby granted to hold to the said Joseph Baron for the lives of William Walter Baron then aged 5¼ years of Mary Baron then aged 8 years and of Elizabeth then aged 6 years son and daughters of the said Joseph Baron.

" Whereas the said Joseph Baron ob. 1 Nov. 1787 having made and published his last Will, dated 30 Octr. 1787 wherein he devised all Freehold and Leasehold to his brother-in-law said Josh. Faulkner Phillips and his friends Richard Kay and Benjamin Potter Upon Trust. Whereas said Thomas Oram did 30 April 1791 Contract and agree with said Executors for the absolute purchase of said Messuage to be mentioned for £483.

G

All that Messuage and Tenement Part R. No. 325 consisting of an house situate in the Market Place in Bury aforesaid containing to the front thereof (exclusive of the Gateway thereunto adjoining) fifteen yards and running in depth backwards from the said front eighteen yards with the Backyard buildings and Stables therein and the Garden containing about (o. o. 6.) of Land or ground of eight yards to the Rod or pole be the same more or less which said Messuage, Garden, and Premises are part and parcel of the same Messuage Dwelling-houses and Hereditaments mentioned to have been devised and granted in and by the Indenture of Lease hereinbefore recited and are now in the tenure and occupation of the said Thomas Oram and his assigns as undertenants with all Houses, Outhouses, Edifices Buildings Barns Stables Yards Orchards Gardens Ways Waters Watercourses Liberties Easements Profits Preveleges Advantages Hereditaments and appurtenances whatsoever to have and to hold for the three lives aforesaid. Paying sd Earl of Derby Yearly Rent £1." The aforesaid Trustees empowered and ordained David Spencer of Bury Shopkeeper and John Salt of Manchester Gentleman their true and lawful attornies to enter in possession of said premises and having obtained quiet possession to deliver the same to him Thomas Oram. Across the deed are signatures and seals of Thomas Falkner Phillips, Richard Kay, Benjamin Potter, and Thomas Oram; witnesses to signatures of Thomas Oram and Thomas Falkner Phillips, Samuel Kay and Charles Wood; witnesses to signature of Benjamin Potter and the receipt of £483, John Kay, attorney, Manchester, and Samuel Kay; peaceable possession given 1797, David Spencer; in the presence of Robert Kay. Besides this deed, the present writer has further perused an abstract of the same deed, passing the same property to Robert Kay, from Thomas Oram, for £400. This latter document is endorsed in the same handwriting as the body of the abstract : " Draft of Assignment of Bulls Head Inn from Thomas Oram to Robert Kay." Some account of subsequent occupier will be given in another chapter, with extract from Robert Kay's private cash book and ledger.

NOTE.—The lady referred to in the opening paragraph of this chapter is Mrs. Samuel Oram, who has kindly donated to Bury Free Library the Bible which belonged first to John Holt, and ultimately to John Kay, the inventor of the fly-shuttle, whose wife was Anne daughter of this John Holt. Mrs. Oram's gift also includes the Ledger of Robert Kay, and his Cash Book and two very interesting historical papers.

BYGONE BURY.

NAMES AND PLACES.

CHAPTER X.

From the *Bury Times*, November 26th, 1898.

THE Kay property, referred to in my last paper, was up to the year 1848 held in trust from year to year, commencing at the death of Robert Kay, inventor of the drop-box, in 1802, to the death of his son-in-law, John Barlow, of Antrobus, county of Chester, in 1848. The management of this property in the old Market Place seems to have been in the hands of Samuel Kay, the son of Robert Kay. Samuel Kay died in the year 1830, having appointed his " nephew, Thomas Oram, and John White-head, of Elton, bleacher, trustees and executors of this my last will and testament."

By the kindness of Mrs. Samuel Oram, late of Beech Hill, in Bury, I am able to give a detailed description of the Old Market Place property. It will be well to mention here that Robert Kay was survived by three children, namely, Lucy, the wife of Thomas Oram, attorney-at-law; Samuel Kay, whose Will I am now referring to; and Dorothy, the wife of John Barlow above-named. Samuel Kay's Will was signed and sealed 4th March, 1830. He died on the 12th March, aged 66, and probate was granted at

Chester, 10th September, 1830. At the time of his death he resided in his "own house;" which, from a sewer rate demand note (fuller in detail than was then customary), I am able to fix at the then number, 44, Fleet Street, Bury.

His Will recites as follows:—"I give devise and bequeath all that my third part or share of and in all those two messuages or dwelling-houses braziers shop hereditaments and premises in the Market Place within Bury aforesaid in the respective possessions of William Parkinson John Kay and Thomas Kay and also all that my third part or share of and in all that the messuage or dwelling-house and premises now in my own possession unto my said sister Lucy Oram for and during the term of her natural life." Here we have names and places as existing in 1830. We see that the property referred to had most probably been the subject of bequest by Robert Kay in 1802; and it is a reasonable inference that Robert Kay added to his property in Fleet Street a third house after the purchase he effected for £400 mentioned in my previous chapter. John Barlow, the husband of Robert Kay's daughter Dorothy, died in 1848, having made a Will, of which Thomas Oram, one of the executors of Samuel Kay's Will was one of the trustees and executors.

The books of account which I have been allowed to examine close about this period, so far as of interest in this series. The tenants in 1848 were Miss Parkinson, Mr. Bromilow, and Mr. Richard Barlow. According to the indenture mentioned in my last chapter, the two messuages named first in Samuel Kay's Will came into possession of Thomas Oram, attorney-at-law, in 1791. In Robert Kay's private ledger, under date March 25th, 1797, I find an entry to credit of Thomas Oram "By a house £400." Lucy, the daughter of Robert Kay, was married to Thomas Oram on or about October 1st, 1789, as is evident from an entry in Robert Kay's private ledger to Mr. Oram's credit. This entry

says (on Cr. side), " Oct. 1, 1789, By Cash given with daughter
Lucy, £50." In 1792 Thomas Oram resided at " Ridivales near
Bury." Samuel Kay kept his accounts in a long parchment-
bound book. Some entries are of interest : " 1803, February 16,
Pd. Mr. Unsworth for probate of father's Will, £11 11s. od."
" 1803, March 30, Paid Lord's rent for my house £0 10s. od. ;
For Tavern £1 os. od." These entries prove that the purchase
which was the subject of the indenture already referred to, and
the rent of which was £1, was added to by a subsequent purchase, the rent of which was 10s. " 1807, May 9, Paid Lord's
rent of my house £0 10s. od. ; For Bull's Head £1." Among
the hundreds of entries perused, I have selected only a few.
There is a statement of account between " Sister Lucy Oram,
Dr., to Saml. Kay," commencing 28th April, 1805, and closing
July 3rd, 1815. Towards the total sum due on account is
entered thus : " Recd. of Sister Oram in rent, household furniture,
and silver tankard ;" followed by the " Balance due to Saml.
Kay. Witness, Thomas Fletcher, July 3rd, 1815, settled." The
special interest attaching to this entry is that this Thomas
Fletcher, a reedmaker, was father of the well-known Dr. Matthew
Fletcher. " 1808, April 19, Recd. from Wm. Parkinson for rent,
£19 10s." " 1808, October 4, Paid Henry Whitehead window
tax 4s. Landlord's duty on my house £1 3s. Do. on Parkinson's £3. Do. on Jardine's £2 4s." I have met with no entries
clearly showing Jardine's tenancy, which appears rented at
£15 15s. for half-year. George Moscrop, Joseph Handley, and
William Parkinson are found paying rent regularly up to about
the year 1840. In that year we have James Handley, Robert
Parkinson, and George Moscrop; in 1841 Robert Parkinson,
G. Moscrop, and Richard Barlow; in 1845 we find Miss Parkinson, Mr. Bromilow, and Richard Barlow ; and the last three
names continue to 1848, when these accounts close, consequent

on the death of John Barlow, of Antrobus, whose wife, as before stated, was Dorothy, the eldest daughter of Robert Kay, the inventor of the drop-box. The final division of the estates of Robert Kay, ob. 1802; Samuel, his son, 1830; John Barlow, above named, 1848; and Lucy Oram, the daughter of Robert Kay, took place on the death of the said Lucy Oram in 1856. The participants were the Winder family of Preston; the White-head family of Elton; four of the first-named family and five of the latter, and Thomas Oram. The Joseph Baron mentioned in the indenture given in my last chapter may have been the husband of Mary Kay, sister of Richard Kay of Baldingstone. One of the trustees of the old chapel at Stand (1713-1736) was a Peter Baron, who " lived at Redivales near Bury." He appears to have been a man of some position in the neighbourhood; but I know no details of his life. One of his daughters married the Rev. Thomas Braddock, first minister of the congregation now meeting in Bank Street Chapel, Bury. (Rev. R. T. Herford's *History of Stand Chapel*).

Robert Kay of the Park near Bury, father of the inventor of the fly-shuttle, had a brother who probably was born at the Park, and who on reaching man's estate, went to Pike Farm. But whether so or not, Thomas Kay, born 1730, of the Pike Farm, claimed to be half-cousin to John Kay the inventor—Thomas's grandfather being brother to the inventor's father, if the claim was well founded. Thomas Kay, born 1730, had a son John, born 1760, who had the Pike Farm after his father. He had also a son, Thomas Kay, born 1758, who on reaching man's estate, went to farm the Knowe, in Tottington. Of twenty-one children born to him, mention may be made of Thomas, who succeeded his father at the Knowe, and, marrying a Miss Heap, had with other children a son, James Kay, who married Mary Hoyle, having with others a son, Thomas Kay, born 1843, now

living in Bury, the father of an only son, John. This information
is derived from statements made by James Kay (born 1804), son
of John Kay, already referred to as born in 1760. James Kay
here named died about twelve years ago, aged 82. In narrating
these old traditions my correspondent says : " I will commence
with a man that my grandfather said was half-cousin to the
inventor, and lived at Pike Farm—Thomas Kay, born about
1730." This correspondent resides in Ramsbottom. We are
thus able to trace back six or seven generations till we come in
line with John Kay the inventor. One of my aims is to prove
unfounded the claim of Thomas Sutcliffe to derive descent from
a Yorkshire family. We find members of the Walmersley family
tenanting Park, Lower Park, Park Wood, The Pike, The Hough
(or " Hoof "), Top-o'-th'-Hill, and Cheswell Farms, between 1700
and the present year. In my next chapter I will give the last
transactions in shuttles which were recorded by the Kays. There
are very few entries made after the death of Robert Kay in 1802.
But the few recorded will be of interest from several points of
view. In addition to the shuttle transactions, I shall be able to
give a few particulars indicating the position in life of Robert
Kay. I believe, furthermore, that I shall be in a position to
state, on good evidence, that the Park Kays, the " Cobbas "
Kays, and the Chesham Kays are all of one stock, which included
the Widdell, the Cheesden, and many other branches.

NOTE.—See Notes to Chapter VII. *ante.*
    The family relationship of the Thomas Kay named in this chapter is
not impugned, as it is well established that there were two brothers of the
inventor's father, all the three brothers being the "lives" included in the
lease granted to their father of Shipperbottom Closes in 1694 by the Right
Hon. the Earl of Derby. This point in the family history has been found
qualified by facts disclosed in the *Memoir of John Kay.*

BYGONE BURY.

I T has been shown in preceding chapters that Robert Kay, joint inventor with his father, was in very prosperous circumstances. He died on the 28th December, 1802. We have seen that Lucy, the youngest of the two daughters who survived him, had, in October, 1789, been married to Thomas Oram, attorney, of Bury. Dorothy, the elder daughter, has been mentioned as having been married to John Barlow of Antrobus, county Chester, yeoman. The author has been favoured by the sexton of the Parish Church of Rostherne, near Knutsford, with a copy of gravestone records relating to burials of the Barlow family, which enable us to fix the year of birth of Dorothy Kay. "Dorothy, the wife of John Barlow, of Antrobus, died January 5th, 1834, aged 75 years;" therefore she must have been born about the year 1759. In her father's ledger an account appears, recording transactions between himself and John Barlow, commencing with the entry, "March 7th, 1798, To Cash paid for Flocks £2 10s.;" followed by an entry June 1st, "Cash £17 10s." Upon the credit side we find—

" 1798, June 1st, By Cash given with daughter Dorothy, £20," which is added to on the 4th September, 6th November, and 13th December of the same year, by payments making up the total " given with Dorothy," to £50. Thus Dorothy was dowered with a like sum to her sister Lucy. Two sons were born of this marriage—William Barlow, born 28th November, 1799, died 9th July, 1810, aged 12 years ; and Robert Kay Barlow, born 29th September, 1802 (namesake of his grandfather Kay), died 27th July, 1847, aged 44 years. From these records we are able to fix the ages of Robert Kay's children in the order of their birth— Dorothy's birth year, 1759; Samuel's 1764; and Lucy's 1770. Lucy was married about the age of 19 ; Dorothy about the age of 39. Dorothy seems to have remained under the parental roof from her mother's death in 1792, for a period of six years. Her father survived his wife about nine years, she having died at the end of January, 1792, and he on the 28th December, 1802.

The first transaction recorded in shuttles recorded by Samuel Kay, after his father's death, was on 30th March, 1803 :—" Sent to James Feltcher, Rochdale, 1 doz. of wheel shuttles at £2 14s." Probably these, at 4s. 6d. each, would be large shuttles for woollen looms. " December 1, 1803, sold George Dickenson, Scoling, near Kendal, 2 wheeled shuttles turned up, at 4s. 6d. ; 2 Dd. D.B. at 4s. 6d. ; 8 Do. Single Heads at 4s. ; £2 10s. Sent by Richard Taylor, Butter Dealer, Westmorland." " February 2, 1804, sold George Dickenson, Scobugh, near Kendal, 24 wheel shuttles at 4s., £4 16s. Sent them by Richard Taylor to be left at John Scott's warehouse, Kendal, Westmorland." April 5 and May 2, same year, sold same man 24 doz. each date, at 4s. 6d. May 17 same buyer 24 doz. without springs at 4s. 4d., and June 15 to same person 48 wheel shuttles at 3s. 10d. each. January 7, 1805, Thomas Wood, brazier, Bolton, is a buyer ; and August 4th also. September 13, 1806, Messrs. Aspenall and

Co., Little Bolton, 34 wheel shuttles turn ups, at 4s. 3d., £7 4s. 6d. August 24, September 7 and 15, 1807, same firm. September 25, 1807, William Booth, Holcom Brook, buys 12 wheel shuttles. March 29th, 1809, William Machin, 6 shuttles at 1s. 10d., No. 12, Nicholas Croft, near Zion Temple, Manchester. April 2, 1810, Messrs. Nailor Aspenall and Co., Little Bolton, 12 wheel shuttles, loose tongs, 3s. 4d., £2. August 10, 1812, sold Joseph Hanson (Bury), 1 wheel shuttle, ordered by James Butterworth on town account, 4s. May 11, 1813, sold James Haslam on town's account 3 wheel shuttles, 11s. 3d. November 18, 1813, to January 3, 1814 inclusive, six sales are entered to Messrs. Nailer and Co. January 12, 1814, sold Richard Greenhalgh (Bury) 2 wheel shuttles for William Eccles, 7s. 6d. Turner's, September 18, 1813, 7s. January 31, sold Richard Greenhalgh 2 wheel shuttles for James Brindle, 7s. 6d. April 26, May 3 and 5 are sales to Richard Greenhalgh for use by Robert Colling, John Rostern, and John Kirkman respectively, 1 pair each, 7s. The last-named pair ordered by note as follows:—" Mr. Kay,—Please to let the bearer Jno. Kirkman have two shuttles, and place them to my account.— Yours, &c., Richard Greenhalgh, Bury, May 5th." On the 13th October ensuing there is an entry, : " Paid Richd. Greenhalgh for the piece of muslin £1 19s." " March 8, 1815, Rich. Greenhalgh 1 w. shuttle for Jon. Wark, 3s. 6d." So ends the business of Samuel Kay's shuttle-making, according to his account book.

In 1816 we find in the *Commercial Directory*, printed by Wardle and Pratt, and published by them and James Pigot, of Manchester—" T. Butterfield, Shuttle Maker, Fleet Street, Bury." In all probability this person succeeded the Kays in their business of shuttle-makers. A few years later we find " James Butterfield, linen draper, and shoe warehouse, Fleet Street," and " Thomas Butterfield, Shuttle Maker, near Stanley Street," which place may really mean the same as stated "Fleet Street" earlier on; for in 1825 another Directory gives "Thomas Butterfield, Shuttle Maker, Fleet Street." With Thomas Butterfield (who doubtless was the son of Henry Butterfield, the husband of Mary, daughter of John Openshaw of Pimhole and his wife Elizabeth, daughter of Oliver Ormerod of Bury) there was as an apprentice James Shepherd, who subsequently had a shuttle business in the Mosses, Bury, as well as a machine business in partnership with John Kay, in the Market Place, Bury. The members of this firm, Kay and Shepherd, were cousins, descendants of the "Cobbas" family. James Shepherd's mother was Ellen Kay of Cobbas; and John Kay, his partner, was son of Ellen's brother Robert. The machine business was not a success; and James Shepherd settled down to his own particular trade, acquired under Thomas Butterfield, as shuttle maker. James Shepherd's descendants are the present business firm of tailors, Mr. Crawshaw of Bury, whose mother, Mrs. Ellen Crawshaw, over eighty years of age, still survives. About the period we refer to, when the shuttle business in the Mosses was prospering, there was in Bury a temple-comb maker, Isaac Wood, who fraternised a good deal with "Jimmy" Shepherd, and by constant association with him acquired a thorough knowledge of shuttle making. Isaac furnished himself with requisite tools, and added the manufacture of shuttles to his own trade of temple-comb making. Having thus facilities for both businesses, he naturally sought for trade wherever he could.

An anecdote is related of his interview with Mr. Thomas Openshaw of Pimhole, the son of "George Openshaw of Seales," who would be cousin to Thomas Butterfield, and was the active partner in the woollen trade of John Openshaw, Son, and Co. Isaac Wood, in his own interest, solicited orders for shuttles at prices considerably below "Jimmy" Shepherd's. Thomas Openshaw listened to all that Isaac could urge in favour of his own shuttles, and then quietly closed the matter by saying : " No, Isaac, not while Jimmy lives." James Shepherd died August 31st, 1849, at the age of 60 ; after which came Isaac's chance. Robert Kay's position in life was one of opulence as wealth was then counted. His private ledger records many transactions which show that he was able to lend money out to rising firms in Bury. In his ledger were found several loose slips of paper, containing particulars of his investments and property. One of these slips contained the following :—" 1798, May 19, money owing me : Messrs. Kay, Baslane, principal and interest, £307 10s. ; Thomas Fletcher, £299 ; Cousin John Kay, £265 ; Thos. Thornley, £51 5s. ; Turnpike, £50 ; Charles Hill, £198 10s. ; R. Battersby, £420 ; Wm. Gee, £20—£1,611 5s. Tavern (Bull's Head), £400 ; my house, £300—£2,311 5s." These investments underwent some changes. A slip dated 1802, the end of which year saw the close of Robert Kay's life, contains the following items under the heading " Money owing me :"— " Cousin J. Kay, principal and interest, abt £287 5s. ; Mr. Thornley, £50 ; Turnpike, £52 10s. ; Charles Hill, £130 ; Battersby, &c., £520 ; Wm. Gee, £20 ; J. Barlow (his son-in-law), £315 ; George Howarth, £300—£1,674 15s. ; tavern and house, £700—£2,374 15s." His ledger contains a few items of historical interest. He enters in Thomas Oram's account, May 28th, 1797, credit for " Brookbottoms last Mich. rent £18 10s." In September, same year, Robert Kay paid Mr. Thremble an account for brandy 5s., wine and bottle 3s. 3d. Loans were made to the undermentioned persons and firms :—Thomas Kent, Manchester, £100. Messrs. James Kay, senr., and Richard Kay, Baslane, 1786, £300, and interest regularly paid for twelve years, when, in November, 1798, the principal was paid back. Robert Kay, Brookshaw, borrowed December 1, 1784, £100, and paid interest yearly, and repaid loan 16th May, 1793. May

30, 1787, Messrs. Law Ormerod, Esq. and Law Shaw, are
borrowers of £110 ; which was paid back, with interest, on September 9, 1789.   On the 1st February, 1786, Robert Kay lent
Thomas Fletcher on "mortgage of sundry property," £350 ;
this was repaid, with interest, on 14th September, 1798.   John
Kay, Redivals, borrowed on the 10th July, 1788, £50 ; repaying
principal and interest 13th July, 1789.   On the 1st of March,
1788, an account was opened, headed "Messrs. Robt. Jno. and
Jno. Kay junior," who borrowed £100.   Interest was regularly
paid up to March 23, 1793, when it seems that John Kay junior
took over the business ; for the names " Robt. Jno. & " are ruled
through, leaving the heading " Jno. Kay, junr."   In May 16th,
1793, a line in the account reads " To Cash, John Kay jun., as
per Note, £100."   Again, November 20, same year, £90 6s.,
and February 3, 1794, a sum of £9 14s. ; making three loans
amounting to £300.   But on 11th July, 1794, a sum of £40
being repaid, the loans became altogether, £260.   On the 1st of
March, 1795, an entry appears :—" N.B.   Note renewed by John
Kay, late of Park."   Thus was the account carried forward to
July 11th, 1797, when it needs must be continued upon a new
page in the ledger.   The heading of this new page reads " Cousin
John Kay, jun."   This account then continues till 11th July,
1802, when it was closed, and new notes given for a fresh account
headed " Mr. John Kay, Park," which was finally closed on
February 9, 1802, by the payment of principal and interest due,
in a bill for £291 4s. 4d., payable two months after date.   The
inventor, Robert Kay, was executor and trustee of James
Fletcher's will, as mentioned in a previous chapter.   An entry,
under date November 8, 1781, appears :—" Received from Rev.
John Smith and Jno. Nuttall remainder due on late Robt. Kay's
of Park Bond £40 ;" from which it would seem that Robert
Kay, of Park, had been some time dead.   Hence, the account

opened with "Robert Jno. and Jno. Kay, jun." March 1st, 1788, was with a Robert subsequent (perhaps son of " late Robert, of Park.") Robert, Kay, whose executors (Rev. John Smith and John Nuttall) paid off the bond, had been a borrower from James Fletcher; to whom the trustee, Robert Kay, may have been nephew. Or the debtor to James Fletcher's estate may have been grandfather to the executor of same, *i.e.*, Robert Kay. I have given these details in order to show relationship between the debtors and Robert Kay. It seems to me that Robert Kay, the father of John the inventor, had sons John and Robert; John, being the inventor, and his brother, Robert, continuing to carry on their father's business, had a son John, whose son, John, would be "Junr." (*vide* cash account of James Fletcher's estate). This seems most probable; for the reason that John Kay (born 1704) had a son John, who married Elizabeth, the daughter of Myles Lonsdall; and, also, the son Robert, whose ledger is now under examination. John Kay the husband of Elizabeth Lonsdall, would be "Junior" to his father; and Robert Kay's "Cousin John Kay," was the son of "John Kay, late of Park," which last-named may have removed from Park about 1795, as above mentioned. On January 29th, 1802 (the year in which Robert Kay the inventor died), he lent Robert Kay of Brookshaw a second loan of £140 on which the interest was regularly paid, and principal repaid 31st January, 1809.

NOTE.—The author having been able to procure correct data as to the relationship of Robert Kay, the executor to his "cousin John Kay," has set the facts out in full in the *Memoir of John Kay*, the inventor of the fly-shuttle. But, leaving the above article to stand as first penned, it is the author's wish to explain the riddle to readers of "Bygone Bury," who may not have access to the *Memoir* named.

The following is the true lineage deduced from the Wills which have disposed of the Park estate from its earliest possession by this family, to its disposal by sale to the Grant brothers.

In 1694 Robert Kay, son of Robert Kay of Sheep-hey, purchased the Park estate, having sons Robert, of whom presently; John, then aged 40; Richard, then aged 35.

Robert Kay the eldest son, born about 1652, had Park estate, and dying in 1704, left four sons in their minority, and a postbumous son was born—the inventor of the fly-shuttle. These five sons were named in the Will. Robert, born 1693, of whom presently; Ephraim, born 1697; Richard; William; and John, the inventor, born 1704, who marrying Annie Holte, had with eleven other children, Robert, the eldest son, who invented the drop box, and who was executor to James Fletcher's Will, referred to in this chapter.

Robert Kay, born 1690, had Park estate, and he had issue by Ann his wife, as per his Will, dated 14th March, 1777, proved 15th May, 1780, four daughters and one son; Ellen, wife of John Nuttall, Top o' th' Lee; Betty, wife of John Taylor; Rachel, wife of James Haworth; Alice, wife of John Kay; and Robert, who was heir to Park Estate and sole executor.

Robert Kay last named, made his Will on 20th May, 1780, which was proved at Chester 18th September, 1780, in which he mentions one daughter the eldest child, and three sons. Of the sons Robert was the eldest, of whom presently; John was the second son; and Richard was the third and last. Each of these sons were left estates.

Robert Kay, the eldest son, had Park estate, and went to reside in Red-vales. His Will is dated 24th March, 1788, and in it he bequeaths Park Estate to his brothers John and Richard in equal shares, John to have the first offer of purchase, paying Richard the moiety due to him on valuation.

The Park estate was thus left in Trust, with the first right of purchase to John, and it seems that neither brother would agree to buy from the other. Richard sold his share and interest to John Lonsdale of Haslingden, and duly conveyed the same to him in fee simple by indenture of lease and re-lease bearing date respectively the 8th and 9th of October, 1792. Now John bought this from John Lonsdale's eldest son by the aid of a certain person named in the deed; and, having married Molly the daughter of Robert Kay of Baslane and his wife Richmal, the daughter of Thomas Kay of Chesham, and dying in 1806, did by his last Will and Testament, and by a Codicil of the said Will bearing date 29th day of July, 1806, appoint his wife Molly and their two sons John Kay and Thomas Kay, executors—gave, devised, and bequeathed the same unto his said wife and children, share and share alike, as tenants in common and not as joint tenants, to be transferred and transferable as they should attain the age of 21 years. Their surviving children were John Kay, Thomas Kay the grocer, Elizabeth Kay, Mary Ann Kay, and Richard Kay, all of whom had attained the age of 21 years.

Ultimately the estate of Park was sold as by deed dated 31st March, 1827, to William Grant and Brothers; parties to that deed being Molly Kay of Bury, widow; Thomas Kay and John Kay of the same place, grocers; Elizabeth Kay and Mary Ann Kay also of Bury, spinsters; and Richard Kay of the same place, grocer [in Union Street].

This is the whole story of the entrance upon and departure from the Park estate of this branch of the Kay family. The present-day representatives of this family are two sons of Richard Kay last named and their children; amongst the latter only one male descendant—John Kay. The cousinship is indicated above.

H

BYGONE BURY.

CHAPTER XII.

From the *Bury Times,* January 21st, 1899.

THERE is one source of information not readily accessible to the general reader from which I may cull a few items of interest—*The Exchequer Lay Subsidy, 1332* : *Wapintachiu de Salfordir,* showing the inhabitants able to aid the Government. Salford, in 1332, had ten such persons and the total of their contributions was xxijs., Blakerode had six who made up ixs., Radecliue had seven who contributed xiiis. iiijd., Oldom had eight subscribing xvjs. iiijd., Bury had eleven who contributed xls., Middelton had nine who contributed xls., Pilkington had nine who contributed xxiiis. iijd.; Totynton had five who contributed xiiijs. The four places last named, especially Bury and Middleton, come out very good, showing that there were some well-to-do families then about Bury. As we are more interested in Bury names and places, I will give full particulars of Bury : Margia de Radcliue vijs., Johe de ffenton iijs., Thom de Werberton ijs. iiijd., Willo Kay iijs. iiijd., Rico de Notehogh ijs., Ad fil Robti vijs., Johe fil Mathi vijs., Rog de Walmeslegh ijs., Willo de Bury ijs. iiijd., Johe de Routesthorn ijs., Willo le Mordmer ijs. Modernised these names are :—Margerie of Radcliffe, John of Fenton, Thomas of Warburton, William Kay, Richard of Nuttall,

Adam son of Robert, John son of Matthew, Roger of Walmersley, William of Bury, John of Rostron, and William the Mortimer. In this list of contributors we find William Kay, who in 1332 was assessed to the Exchequer at the yearly sum of iijs. iiijd. (3s. 4d.) This is evidence of considerable wealth. It is to be remembered that the country, extending north from Manchester to Pendle Hill was probably one great forest, with only residential property here and there, the seats of the proprietors or larger vassals, under the great tenants of the Duchy. The writer's present purpose is to follow the fortunes of the Kay families. In 1332 William Kay is the only resident of rank of that name about Bury. Three generations after the period named the royal forests of Rossendale were deforested by Royal Warrant. Before this came to pass families had already possessed themselves of clearings in and around the forests, which extended to, and included, "Totynton," and no doubt approached Bury in the easterly direction. In 1538 Parish Registers were, by royal injunction, ordered to be kept by all parochial clergy. There were no Nonconformists' chapels in those early times. All christenings, burials, and weddings were to be recorded in a parish book, kept by the clergy of the several parishes. The register kept by the clergyman of the parish of Bury commenced with the year 1590. A transcript of the registers of the Parish Church of Bury, published by the Lancashire Parish Register Society, and printed by permission of the Rev. Foster Grey Blackburne, Rector of Bury and Hon. Canon of Manchester, has just been issued to the members of the society. I observe with regret the poor interest taken in this subject by people in and around Bury. The list of members of the society includes Heywood Free Library, Bolton Free Library, Manchester Free Library, Atkinson Free Library, Southport, Barrow Free Library, Birkenhead Free Library, Boston Free Library,

Chetham's Library, Manchester, Leeds Free Library, Liverpool Free Public Libraries, New England Historic Genealogical Society, Boston, U.S.A., New York State Library, Oldham Free Library, Pennsylvania Historical Society, Philadelphia, Pa., U.S.A., Rochdale Free Public Library, St. Helens Free Library, Wigan Free Library. But the Bury Athenæum and the Bury Co-operative Society are both conspicuous by their absence from the list of membership. These omissions are certainly very remarkable, to say the least.

I will pass from this point to refer to some interesting gleanings I have made from the first volume of the Lancashire Parish Register Society. The Bury registers open 5th October, 1590. The christenings are first, burials next, and weddings last. The first christening was James, sonne of Ryc Rothwell, October 5, 1590; the first burial, Robert Wardleworthe, Marche 23, 1590-1; the first wedding, Mathewe Birrie cu vxor Februarie 19, 1590-1. In October, 1590, children christened were sons or daughters of Ryc Rothwell, Edmund Barlowe, George Holilee, John Lomax, John Holte, Rauffe Holte, John Haworthe, Henry Nuttall, John Grinehalghe, and John Lea. It is in " Januarii " following that we find the first christening of a Kay. " Thomas " s. of Ryc Kaye, Januarii 10, 1590-1, and in the following two months, John s. of John Kaye, Februarie 21, 1590-1; James s. of James Kaye, Marche 7, 1590-1; Ellen d. of Edmund Kaye, Marche 9, 1590-1. Then follow six months in which Kays are absent. But they are well represented in the next following month, October : Roger s. of Roger Key, October 3, 1591; James s. of James Kaye, October 10, 1591; Alis and Margret d. of Thomas Kaye, October 17, 1591; Thomas s. of Thomas Kaye, October 24, 1591; Margret d. of Denys Kaye, October 31, 1591. I will just add the remainder of Kays born 1591—Margret d. of Ryc Kaye, December 5, 1591; Alis d. of John Kaye, Januarie 25, 1591-2;

John s. of Thomas Kaye, Februarie 6, 1591-2 ; Robte s. of
Willme Kay, March 12, 1591-2. In the following year, 1592,
christenings are registered of children born to Roberte Key,
Willme Kaye, Ryc Keye, Edward Key, Thomas Kaye, and Robert
Keye. It is quite conceivable that the last two christenings,
which happened on the same day, were distinguished from each
other by the variation in spelling in the record, in accordance
with the parents' request. This variableness runs through the
record—Kay, Kaie, Kaye, Keie, Key, Keye. This diversity
could have been obviated, by the residence of the parents being
entered upon the register. But the ignorance and suspicion of
the people probably prevented this. It was at first imagined
that Parish Registers were ordered so that the governing authority
could more readily follow the people for the purpose of taxation.
Hence all early registers are of very little use for purposes of
genealogical research. But our first volume, *The Registers of the
Parish Church of Bury* (to be immediately followed by a second
volume of the series, *The Registers of Burnley Parish Church*), is
with all the shortcomings peculiar to these early registers, still
helpful and interesting. The foregoing extracts give us names of
a dozen families of the Kays residing in Bury, 1590-1591. I
have gone through the whole of the registers for all of the name
of Kay and its variants. There were 94 marriages of Kays in
the period 1590-1616 registered at Bury ; 46 of these were males,
and 48 females. There were in the same period, 223 children of
the name of Kay and its variants christened, of whom 122 were
boys and 101 girls. During the period named there were 191
burials of Kays, at the Parish Church, inclusive of 50 wives.

In the course of time the registration went more into detail.
From 1590 to 1599 the weddings were recorded with vexatious
brevity, thus the first wedding in 1590-1, which, notably, was a
descendant of the old Bury family, reads, " Matthew Birrie cu

vxor Februarie 19, 1590-1." Then we have a breathing time—
no more till Auguste, when we read, "Thomas Allens cu vxor,
Auguste 9, 1590-1 ; Thomas Kaye cu vxor, Auguste 10, 1590-1 ;
James Fenton cu vxor Auguste 15, 1590-1 ; Ryc Grinehalghe cu
vxor, Auguste 20, 1590-1. But, by carefully comparing christenings, births, and weddings I have been able to put in brief
pedigree form names and places for thirty families of Kays.
Kay, Christopher, died at Bodenstone, buried 6th October, 1591.
This will be identified as Baldingstone. My notion is there was
a wayside stone somewhere about this place, whereon weary
travellers rested, or "bode" for a time, till by rest they were able
to pursue their toilsome journey. Christopher Kay's wife died a
few days prior to her husband, and was buried 26 September,
1591. Their sons, James and Robert, are named. James's
three children were James, christened 30 December, 1596;
Margret, 27, June, 1602; William, 19 March, 1614-15. Then
we have Thomas Kay of Sheephey; "a childe" buried 11 March,
1592-3, and "a sonne" buried 20 February, 1597-8. John Kay,
Top Royle, his wife, buried in 1593, a child 27 September, 1605;
John Kay, Widdell, "a sonne" buried 13th April, 1597, and a
son; Richard Kay married to Elizabeth Cowap 24 February,
1611-12. Robert Kay of Bent had "a child buried, 2 February,
1608, and Alissa, a daughter, buried 30 March, 1611." I surmise his wife was "Alis Nuttall." "Robert Kay and Alis
Nuttall," are registered as married June 22, 1607. Robert Kay
of Bentley Lee, buried children in 1610, 1613, and 1615. Ann,
the wife of Thomas Kay of Bentley Lee, was buried October 1,
1614. Richard Kay de Redivalls buried a son Richard, and a
son William, both on the 22nd December, 1609. He had a
second son Richard, born 1614, and a son Thomas, born 1616.
I may say here, it was not at all unusual, if a child died, to repeat
the same Christian name when subsequent children of the same

sex were christened. A case within my own knowledge was where the parents desired to have a son named a particular name, and I know personally the case where the third son of the same Christian name survives! He has the register showing that he has had two brothers both named John, who preceded him, and died in their infancy; and I have copy of this register. Roger Kay of Shiplebothom has a daughter registered as christened and buried on 25 March, 1609-10; and a brother Robert married 16 September, 1606. The wife of Ryc Kay of Gooseford, was buried 15 December, 1591; Renold Kay of More Yate was buried 17 November, 1616; Ryc Kay de Burrowes (Burrs) buried his wife 21 February, 1591-2; Edmond Kay de Burrowes, buried a daughter 1 January, 1614-15; Roger Kay de Brodcar buried children, Roger in 1615, and Anne in 1616. Owyn Kay de Litlewoode, was buried 31 July, 1592; Rauffe Kay de Cockey buried his wife 1 August, 1592; Roger Kay de Birkle buried his wife Jane 25 November, 1614; Thomas Kay de Bridhole buried his wife Ann, 13 December, 1613; and himself was buried 6 December, 1614. His son Thomas married Emory Leache, 15 September, 1614; and his son Roger had a son christened 1 January, 1614-15. John Kaie de Woodrode, 1612; Richard Kay, Titch Road, 1610; Arthur Kay of Hough, 1613; James Kay of Bentley Lum, 1613; all married. Wm. Kay of Cobas married Dority Barlowe, November 5, 1616. There was a christening of Dorathie d. Robte Barlowe, Januarie 12, 1594-5. These dates of William Kay and his wife, Dorothy, are confirmed by gravestone in the Bury Parish Churchyard.

NOTE.—In 1650 there were only twenty-four families in Shuttleworth, according to the Church Survey. The population of Bury was then less than 2,000.

The foregoing chapter was the author's effort to interest Bury readers in the publications of the Lancashire Parish Register Society, so ably supported by Mr. Henry Brierley, and the Rev. W. J. Löwenberg, both then resident in Bury.

BYGONE BURY.

CHAPTER XIII.

From the *Bury Times*, December 27th, 1902.

FOUR years intervened and the author once more took up the story of John Kay of Bury which was again brought before Bury readers, and Colonel Sutcliffe's fictions once again made to appear facts. This notice of the " Lancashire Worthy " induced the author to return to his self-imposed task of disproving the claims of this man. The facts of the case are that Colonel Sutcliffe in his *Crusoniana*, and also in his lecture in the south of England two years before he died, belies his Bury ancestry. He published a pedigree chart in his *Crusoniana*, which was to exhibit his claims to have descended from Sutcliffes of Stansfield Hall, Todmorden, on the one side, and from Sir John Kaye of Woodsome, Co. York, on the other side. This publication attracted the notice of the late Mr. James Crossley, F.S.A., a well-known Manchester antiquary.

It so happened that Mr. James Crossley had some knowledge of the family of Sutcliffe of Burnley, from whom the Colonel acknowledged himself to have sprung. The Colonel's proclivities led him further afield for some family of more ancient lineage, and he fixed upon Dr. Matthew Sutcliffe, Dean of Exeter (1550-

1629), whose brother John should stand as progenitor for him, the Colonel. It will be seen, when investigation is made by any curious inquirer, that Dr. Matthew Sutcliffe represented a Devonshire family, which had not the remotest connection with the Sutcliffes of Stansfield Hall, Todmorden. The Thomas Sutcliffe of Burnley, acknowledged by the Colonel as his grandfather, moved to Water Lane, Salford, where he carried on his business of dyer and presser. And John Sutcliffe, his son, married Frances, the daughter of John Kay and Elizabeth Lonsdall. The only child of this marriage was Thomas Sutcliffe, born May 13th, 1791—the said Colonel. The Colonel's grandfather, Thomas Sutcliffe, was first cousin to Mr. James Crossley's grandmother, the wife of Henry Crossley. These Sutcliffes were settled at the Ing, near Colne. Mr. James Crossley has left his opinion on record :—" The Colonel's descent from the Sutcliffes of Stansfield is all fudge, for Mrs. Pickup was the first cousin of my grandmother, Martha Crossley, who was the daughter of Ann Sutcliffe, of the Ing, near Colne, who must have been the sister of Colonel Sutcliffe's great-grandfather, Thomas Sutcliffe, who would be of the Ing also, and not of Stansfield. The Colonel's pedigree is as arrant a piece of manufacture as any of the goods his grandfather pressed and dyed." Mrs. Pickup, named here, was sister to the Colonel's grandfather.

Then, as to the Kay descent, as claimed by Colonel Sutcliffe. To make names and dates fit his purpose he fixes upon Sir John Kaye of Woodsome, near Huddersfield, born 1578, who died in 1641, having married Anne, daughter of Sir John Fearne, and had issue a son, Sir John Kaye, created baronet 1641, and died 25th July, 1662, having married Margaret, daughter of Thomas Moseley, leaving a son John, his heir, and a second son Robert. This second son, Robert Kaye, is by the Colonel planted at Park, Walmersley, near Bury, and made to seem father of John

Kay, the inventor of the fly-shuttle. Moreover, this Robert Kaye of Woodsome, is given a wife, by name Mary Crompton. This is the Robert Kay who is said to have been concerned in introducing the stuff trade into Leeds in 1713, and who died in 1727. Reference to the Woodsome pedigree will show that this Robert Kaye died unmarried. Reference to the Will of Robert Kay of Park, Walmersley, will show that the mother of the inventor was Ellen Entwistle of Quarlton, and that the father of the inventor died in 1704, two months before the inventor was born. It seems high time to clear the names of John Kay and his son Robert from all the opprobrium resulting from Colonel Thomas Sutcliffe's fictitious, if not fraudulent, statements.

Once for all let it be closely recognised that the inventor of the fly-shuttle was a Kay of Bury, and the author affirms that there is no " reason to believe that Robert Kay had an association [if the descent from Woodsome is implied], which antedated by several years at least the birth of the inventor, with the woollen Riding of Yorkshire."

The Robert Kaye of Woodsome who was, in his time, concerned with the woollen trade of Yorkshire, was Robert, the son of George Kaye of Woodsome, who is stated to have been a ". merchant." Singular to say this Robert Kaye also died unmarried. His brother, Sir John Lister Kaye, was a prominent Yorkshireman. The George Kaye here named was second son of Sir John Kaye, whom the Colonel would have us think the elder brother of Robert Kay of Park. George Kaye was younger brother to Sir Arthur Kaye, the last male descendant of the main line of Woodsome. Sir Arthur Kaye left an only child, Elizabeth, who was twice married, first to William, second Earl Dartmouth, and second to Lord North, first Earl of Guilford. Colonel Sutcliffe, under date January 25th, 1843, wrote to the Earl of

Dartmouth, and accompanied his letter with the portrait of John
Greenhalgh of Brandlesome, on the back of which he wrote, " I
have traced the descent of John Kay of Bury, from his ancestors
Sir John and Lady Annie Kay of Woodsome." The Earl
replied on the following day, saying " the descent of your relatives
from the Woodsome family of Kayes, seems to be clearly traced."
Note the Colonel's spelling here, " Kay," and the Earl's " Kayes."
If the Colonel's pretensions had been well founded, the Earl
would not have said the descent " *seems* to be clearly traced."
The Colonel's great-grandfather, Robert Kay of Park, would
have been uncle to Sir Arthur Kaye, the last male representative
of Woodsome. And John Kay, the inventor, would have been
cousin, only once removed, to Eizabeth, Viscountess Lewisham ;
afterwards Countess of Guilford. She died 21st April, 1745.
William, fourth Earl of Dartmouth, born 1784, died 1853.
Francis, sixth Earl of Guilford, in holy orders, born 19th
December, 1792, died 29th January, 1861. To these two noblemen Colonel Sutcliffe ought to have been well-known. Baines,
in 1825-6, included John Kay among his names of " Lancashire
Worthies," and it was no longer counted disgraceful to have
family connections between the nobility and eminent men in
trade when the Colonel returned from his wild adventurous life
to his native country. He was in the same line of descent from
Robert Kay of Park that the Earls of Dartmouth and Guilford
were from the Kayes of Woodsome ; and if his pretensions were
well founded, they would have been acknowledged by these
eminent noblemen.

Sutcliffe says : " The Right Honourable Francis North, first
Earl of Guilford (who had married [1736] a relative of Mr. Kay),
did interest himself, as well as the Right Honourable Lord
Strange, but before anything could be done for that Lancashire
worthy he died in Paris, a victim of national ingratitude, and left

his unfortunate family not only to bewail the fate of their parent, but also to experience the taunts of their relatives, as well as the vicissitudes of an adverse fortune." The death of John Kay, in Paris, occurred in 1767 or 1768. The first Earl of Guilford was born in 1704, the same year as the inventor of the fly-shuttle, and in 1736 married Elizabeth, the widow of Viscount Lewisham. This Elizabeth and the inventor of the fly-shuttle would, if Colonel Sutcliffe is believed, be related. Sir Arthur Kaye, her father, would be first cousin to the inventor of the fly-shuttle. It is not unreasonable to find that Sir Robert Peel, whose family was also mixed up by Sutcliffe in his pedigree, turned a deaf ear to the adventurer's supplications for public money to be dispensed " to the poor relations " of the inventor. Naturally Sir Robert Peel might be supposed to reason that claims bolstered up by such fictions as Colonel Sutcliffe had the effrontery to attempt to palm upon him were not worthy of notice. He wrote three times to Sir Robert Peel; who, replying to the second application, said : " I regret that I do not feel myself justified in making any grant of public money on account of the circumstances stated in your letter." This reply is dated 5th December, 1842. In May of the following year Sutcliffe again tried Sir Robert Peel, by reason that a grandson of Hargreaves, the inventor, had obtained from the Royal Bounty £250 for his grandmother, Mrs. Thompson of Manchester. No notice was taken of this. Sutcliffe again wrote, June 24th, and received a reply dated the 30th:—" Sir Robert Peel regrets that he does not feel himself justified in complying with the application referred to in your letter."

That Colonel Sutcliffe had good reason to be proud of his great-grandfather's achievements and inventive genius no one will doubt. The Kays of Walmersley have no need to be ashamed of their progenitors. The first of that name to be found in this

district was William Cay, or Kay, one of the three persons in
Bury of sufficient position to be called upon to pay the Subsidy
of the Crown in 1332.   The descent is good enough, had the
Colonel only known of it, without seeking in Yorkshire for what
had no connection whatever with his family's past.   In his
account of the earthquake of Juan Fernandez, 19th February,
1835, he writes: " I lost nearly everything I had; but, at the
risk of my life, saved my writing-desk, a box with papers, and two
family portraits—Governor Greenhalgh of Brandlesome Hall,
and John Kay, Esq., of Bury, Lancashire, inventor of the fly-
shuttle, &c."   His grandmother was Elizabeth, daughter of
Miles Lonsdall and his wife Elizabeth, daughter of Thomas
Greenhalgh of Brandlesome, sheriff of Lancashire in 1668-9,
ob., 1672.   Colonel Sutcliffe died of heart disease, 22nd April,
1849, aged 59 years, at 357, Strand, London, where for the three
years preceding his death he had subsisted upon the charity of
his landlord, who, at the inquest held upon the deceased, stated
that he was hoping to be recouped by proceeds of a book the
Colonel had completed, but could not produce funds to publish,
when death removed him.   His grandparents had both long
been dead.   Dr. Matthew Fletcher of Bury survived, being the
grandson of Lettice, the eldest daughter of the inventor.   Lucy
Kay, the wife of the first Thomas Oram, survived, and would be
nearly 80 years old.   She was the daughter of Robert Kay,
inventor of the drop-box.   A memorial window to her memory
is placed in Elton Church.   Her daughter Elizabeth married the
elder John Whitehead of Lowercroft, and their sons John and
Robert Kay Whitehead survived.   The elder of these, John, is
represented by our esteemed townsman, Mr. Henry Whitehead
of Haslam Hey, and his brother, Dr. Walter Whitehead, the
celebrated surgeon of Manchester.   Mr. Robert Kay Whitehead
died 20th February, 1900.

If the people of Bury desire worthily to commemorate the bi-centenary of the birth of John Kay, the inventor of the fly-shuttle, who are so likely to lend their aid and patronage, if fittingly approached, as these worthy descendants of that " Lancashire Worthy " and his son Robert ? The firm of Messrs. Hall have set an example of earnestness. If the working people of Bury come forward with their subscriptions, a scholarship could be founded in connection with our High School, now to be open to all. And gold medals might be a yearly institution as recognition of excellence in pursuit of knowledge connected with the textile industry at our Technical School.

BYGONE BURY.

CHAPTER XIV.

From the *Bury Times*, February 21st, 1903.

FINALLY, as matters of further interest the author returned to the earlier history of John Kay of Bury, showing that he was born at Park, 16th July, 1704. His father was dead on the 18th of the month of April previous, comparatively early in life, for none of his sons were arrived at manhood. The Park estate, which he describes as his " freehold inheritance, and the Shupple-bottom Close held by indenture of lease under the Earle of Derby," were assigned to Robert, the eldest son, charged with payment of £30 apiece to each of his younger brothers, including the then unborn brother John. And if any of the four younger brothers died, the shares they would have been entitled to were to be divided among the survivors younger than Robert, " he himself receiving no benefit thereby." Provision in case of the wife's death was made in this wise : Robert, the eldest son, was to pay yearly twenty shillings for Richard's maintenance till he was eighteen years of age ; and to William forty shillings towards his maintenance till he was eighteen ; and " if the infant which is yett to bear do live " after Robert was one-and-twenty years of age, " that he pay it forty shillings a year till it be eighteen

year of age." "The ordering and tuition of my children unto
Ellin, my wife, till they be fourteen years of age." He ordered
his executors to be careful in looking to and preserving all the
younger timber and trees, "the best that they can for the use
and behoof of Robert my son." Ellin, however, married a second
time one Hamer before her two younger sons attained their full
age of twenty-one. And we find William became a shoemaker
in Bury, and John became a reedmaker—and the inventor.

From the extracts here given from Robert Kay's Will, it is
not evident that great wealth existed in that family. The inventory comprised thirty-five moneyed items amounting to £82
13s. 6d., of which one item alone was "Mele £15;" another
item "Four oxen £11 0s. 0d.;" "the hay and straw in the
barne, total, £2 15s. 0d.;" "one mare and colt £5 0s. 0d." "In
the great house — six chears, six cushions, two little chears,
00.08.00;" "saddle and pillion 00.05.00." These items are
selected from the sworn inventory proved with the Will of Robert
Kay, May 27th, 1704. We may estimate the difference in value
of money between that period and now. Forty shillings yearly
till William and the inventor were eighteen was all the provision
charged upon Robert, the eldest born, to come out of the farm,
to support these younger children. Robert the eldest was born,
I believe, about 1690, and so at his father's death would be
about 14 years of age.

Two old Bibles handed down to posterity in the inventor's
family, and purchased by the late Mr. Samuel Oram at the sale
of the household goods of the late Dr. Matthew Fletcher, afford
a little evidence of connection between the Kays of Chamber
Hall and the family which settled at Park. One of these Bibles
contains a record that at one time it was "John Holt's Book."
Anne, the daughter of this John Holt, was married to John Kay
the inventor. But I am of opinion that James Kay was uncle

to the inventor, and had for his second wife Margaret, sister to
this John Holt.   This certainly lends support to Colonel Thomas
Sutcliffe's statement, that the inventor "married a relative."
And this family of Kays at Chamber Hall also seems to have
been associated with the Park Kays, according to Colonel
Sutcliffe's assertion (made without reference to any authority),
to the effect that John Kay became so impoverished by litigation
with the Shuttle Clubs that he had to dispose of his landed
estates near Bury, part of which were even the very ground upon
which the Peel family amassed their wealth.   But the inventor
has never been shown to have had any property at Park, or elsewhere—his elder brother hired Park.   However these families
were connected, it seems, up to the present time, to have been
quite impossible to ascertain.   That they were connected is
almost proved by the two old family Bibles.   One, 1599, seems
to contain John Holt's figuring 1709—1599—110, showing the
family ownership had endured for 110 years.   This family of
Kays at Chamber were connected with the family at Top-o'-th'-
Hill, and also with Robert Nuttall, merchant, of Bury, the pur-
chaser of Bridge Hall estate in 1736, who married Susannah,
sister of James Kay, of Chamber Hall, who nominated his
brother-in-law executor of his Will.

   We now come to a period in the life of the inventor, John
Kay, when it becomes feasible to account for the assertion made
by Woodcroft that "he was educated abroad."   His widowed
mother and her brother William were guardians to the children
at Park.   When the inventor reached the age of eight years his
elder brother Robert would have entered into possession of the
"freehold inheritance."   The widowed mother would remain at
Park in care of the younger children, and probably Robert and
his brothers would go into some trade, as well as attend to the
farm.   But their family connections, merchants and dealers with

I

combed and carded wool and yarn, were constantly dealing with
Dutch merchants abroad; and in those days, as now, it would
be quite possible to get children into convent schools. We know
from evidence of his after life, and from family traditions, that
the Park Kays were Jacobites, and mixed up in the latest
Pretender's escapades in Manchester, in 1745. Then we will
assume that he was taken abroad by some family acquaintances,
and placed out in some family with whom these family acquaintances had dealings; and so had opportunity of obtaining his
education. But this is surmise only. Returning home, when he
had attained the age of fourteen, he would be (in fact, family
tradition comes in again, and says he was) put to learn the trade
of a reedmaker. He probably, in rather a restive spirit, followed
this trade, and served his term of apprenticeship. But once
again we will accept evidence from tradition, to the effect that
he rebelled against his appointed master, and returned home,
saying he "could learn nothing there." His active brain was
thus soon at work—they could teach him nothing. Doubtless
he had seen cane-split reeds in plenty while on the Continent, if
not about Bury, before and after his Continental experiences.

In the writer's view John Kay had seen something in wire,
and the possible uses of it. In early times wire was all drawn
down by the hammer, and, when down to 1-16th inch square,
could be drawn by hand round hat-shaped wire blocks fixed upon
upright spindles. In fact, it is only within a very few years,
within the author's knowledge, that small sizes of brass, copper,
silver, and gold wire were all drawn by hand power.

John Kay wanted to be rid of cane splits, so as to obtain an
easier run for the shuttle; and a more even beat-up of the weft,
and he would try his hand at some flattened wire. No. 16
wire was then considered a standard 1-16th of an inch in
diameter, if of round wire. But we will not go over the ground

BYGONE BURY. 115

of wire-drawing. We fancy he got a ring or two of No. 16 wire, and by some method, probably hand-hammering, flattened it down to ⅛in. wide, when it would make dents broad enough and thin enough to compete with smooth cane dents. The hammering being carefully done, the edges would be rounded pretty evenly if the material used was of good Swedish charcoal-iron, such as for centuries has been in vogue for horse-shoe nails. He was successful. His dents were ready; but flattened wire patented was not much good to him so far. So he did not patent it. He saw at once he could have firm, even, flat-wire dents; that what he next must have, would be most even cording, or twine, twisted as beautifully and regularly in its threads as possible. So he set about his machine to obtain these results. He found mohair suitable, and that he could make strong thread. He then sought for a patent for "Thread, &c.," his first patent, 1730.

If the inventor had set the public mind upon a patent for making "Reed-twine," his chance was gone. So we find his first patent was for twisting mohair and finishing tailors' thread. His reeds are now ready. Some are being tried. "The reed face," said he, "is as smooth and even as it is possible." What about improving the loom to get the best results? "Why," said he to himself, "the slay-beam only needs a bit at each end added, to catch the shuttle, and jerk it from side to side; for the reed is so even now, on the face, compared with the old cane reeds, if I can get a shuttle-box at each end of the slay I can tie the strings to a ' picker,' and both strings to a peg for the right hand, and the weaver will have the left hand to beat up the slay regularly; and if he goes all right with his clogs on the treadles, he may soon be at it, ricketty, racketty, the day through!" And so it came out just as he imagined. But the first man who was dispensed with was probably the first growler

over the patent of 1733. A superficial observer would perhaps
now remark, " it's all very simple." So it is, and so was the first
spoon formed out of boxwood, or bog-oak, when people grew out
of using their fingers at dinner or other feeding times.

John Kay's reed yarn, and perhaps reedmaking, led him to
Colchester, where weaving was a great source of work. He
tried, no doubt, to push his reeds and yarns, with some success.
But he found proposals on foot to supply the town with water,
and no mechanical appliances suitable. He thought this matter
over. Probably one sleepless night he tumbled to the plan to
adopt. The wind blew wheresoever it listed. And so it was—
1738, a patent windmill suitable to convey power for many
purposes.

It has been a myth all through the records of Kay's early life,
that he went to Colchester to look after the works his father had
there; and that his father dying in 1727, as Colonel Sutcliffe
told the world, the son remained ten years longer to carry on the
concern! Most probably the truth was he only made occasional
journeys to Colchester.

John Kay married Anne Holt in 1725. He had come to the
age of one-and-twenty years, and was entitled to the legacy in
his father's Will. We can, consequently, suppose he got his £30
or £40. Perhaps with savings he had acquired, and help from
his father-in-law, he struck out for himself.

Dr. Laver, antiquary, of Colchester, wrote to the author some
years ago, that he had searched all the likely Church registers
there, but found no records of any christenings of children born
to John Kay of Bury, or of Colchester. Up to present date
records have only been found at Bury Parish Church, and the
first there is the christening of Lettice, daughter of John Kay,
born July 11th, and christened July 13th, 1726. No place of
residence is given. But it is unquestionable, the writer thinks,

that this child is identical with the " Lettice Fletcher " whose burial is recorded on the Fletcher family gravestone in Bury Churchyard, south side. The writer has only identified three christenings described as " of Park." The first one is " Ephraim s. of Robt. Kay de Park, born May 7, bapd. May 9, 1697;" second, " John s. Robert Kay, Park, born July 16, baptd. July 23, 1704;" third (which indicates the period in life when the eldest son, Robert, was married), " Elizab. d. Robert Kay, Park, b. Jany. 30, baptd. Feby. 9, 1723." This entry indicates that the christening in 1690 of Robert, s. of Robert Kay (no residence given), born September 28, and baptised October 2, was that of the said eldest brother of the inventor, who must have married as soon as he attained the age of twenty-one years. But further search has resulted in finding the inventor's other children, numbering twelve, as shown in the *Memoir* now published.

At this point friends begun to urge that the author's collection of material should assume book form. Hence *Memoir of John Kay* offered by subscription; and this volume of *Bygone Bury*, in which, obviously, there are many things duplicated, but circumstances appeared to require the repetitions.

JAMES CLEGG
· PRINTER ·
Rochdale

CPSIA information can be obtained
at www.ICGtesting.com
Printed in the USA
BVHW030859210819
556415BV00009B/858/P

9 789389 450743